Out of Time:

Surviving the Sixties

By James P. MacGuire

Other Books by James P. MacGuire:

London and the English Countryside

Campion (with Christopher Buckley)

Beyond Partisan Politics

Miracle in East Harlem: The Fight for Choice in Public Education (with Seymour Fliegel)

Dusk on Lake Tanganyika and Other Poems

The Rockaway Hunting Club at 125 (with Dr. Benjamin Allison)

Newman and the Intellectual Tradition

The Catholic Shakespeare?

Modern Science/ Ancient Faith

The Catholic William F. Buckley Jr.

Catholicism and the American Experience

Real Lace Revisited

Worlds Within Worlds: A Father's Poems and Prayers

Table of Contents

I.	Preface 1960-66	8
II.	Fall 1966	59
III.	1967	87
IV.	1968	129
V.	1969	177
VI.	1970	237
	Epilogue	312
Acknowledgements		331
Author's Biography		332

For Hilary Martin, O.S.B.

Out of Time:

Surviving the Sixties

When you ain't got nothing, you got nothing to lose—

    Bob Dylan
    ("Like a Rolling Stone")

Out of Time: *Surviving the Sixties*

I. Preface: 1960-1966

1.

The 1960s started out slowly and serenely, then gathered steam and ended in a frenzy of anger and regret. Those who remember the decade fondly grope for words like "intense" to praise it. But for many like me the overriding recollection is one of confusion.

I was seven when they started and eighteen when they ended, traversing a time from the second grade to the cusp of college.

The 1960s accelerated from something close to stasis to the speed of a particle collider.

Our parents' generation had come back from World War II not wanting to talk about it, going to work and quietly getting on with their lives. Nothing much happened in the 1950s compared to the War. By comparison to what they had seen and done, that was fine by them.

My father had joined the Squadron A Cavalry fresh out of Yale, and was due to be discharged three days after Pearl Harbor on December 7th, 1941. After the sneak attack, he immediately volunteered for the Air Force and learned how to fly in Texas before shipping out for the Pacific, where, based on the tiny atoll of Attu at the end of the Aleutian chain, he lost several colleagues who smacked their planes into the steep mountain side that loomed menacingly at the end of the short air strip. My mother thought he may have had a nervous breakdown there, because he was sent to the mainland of Alaska for a month of R&R. For decades after his sleep was bedeviled by a nightmare in which the island was socked in as he was trying to land, and Dad repeatedly cried out, "I can't see!"

My brothers and I went to the Lawrence School on the South Shore of Long Island, one of the country day schools founded by B. Lord Buckley, the educational entrepreneur, along with Buckley, Buckley Country Day, and Greenvale.

In the Fall of 1960, entering the third grade and ascending from the "Primary" to the "Junior" department, we donned coats, ties and exquisitely uncomfortable Oxford shoes, which at least in my case were all more or less permanently askew. We played our first six man football game against East Woods and lost 40-0. When in the rematch we narrowed the margin to 20-0, our Headmaster, Mr. Barber, hailed it in assembly as "a moral victory."

Enthusiasm might have been Mr. Barber's middle name. His name was Anthony Victor Barber, and he wore a gold tie clasp with the initials "AVB." If one asked him what that stood for, he would look somewhat pained and then confess, "A Very Bad Boy." He stood in the front hallway of the Hewlett Bay Park campus every morning and firmly shook the hand of every student who entered, looked them straight in the eye, addressed them by name, and expected them do the same in return. Morning assemblies included band presentations of variable tunefulness, the Pledge of Allegiance, readings from Scripture, the Lord's Prayer, a hymn or two ("One World Built on a Firm Foundation," "No Man is an Island," and the Navy Hymn were all perennials), capped by congratulations on what had been accomplished and an exhortation to do even better, always in Mr. Barber's booming voice.

He retired to Tuxedo Park in 1963, when my class was finishing fifth grade, and since I was living out of the country for some years after college I had no contact with him for well over a decade. One day in the early 1980s I ducked out of the Time-Life building on Sixth Avenue and raced over to the Racquet Club for a noontime squash game. As I was changing in one of the dressing room cubicles a voice rang out, "Good morning."
"Good morning," I muttered, rushing to my court.
"I SAID 'GOOD MORNING' MR. MacGUIRE."
Startled, I looked up. He was dressed in immaculate white flannels, having finished his morning court tennis doubles match. He was well

into his 80s by then but still vigorous. I sputtered my apologies for not recognizing his voice at once, and he let me off with a relatively gentle needle: "Didn't I hear that you spent a year or two at Cambridge after finishing Hopkins?"

"Yes sir, Mr. Barber."

"Not bad," he allowed with a sly smile. Tony was proud of being an Oxford man.

1960 was the year the Mau Mau rising ended in Kenya and no fewer than seventeen African countries gained their independence. Construction on the Aswan High Dam began in Egypt. The payola scandal erupted over radio disc jockeys accepting money in return for playing particular records. In February, goalie Jack McCarten led the US team to the hockey goal medal at the Squaw Valley Olympics. I was playing soccer on a chilly afternoon at the little field on the Isle of Wight, a residential backwater up against the marshlands in Lawrence, and when my Dad picked me up we listened in his station wagon, our excitement building, to the last minutes of the game. In March of that year Lucille Ball filed for divorce from Desi Arnaz after nineteen years of marriage, ending not only the Lucy franchise but our fond hopes they would buy an east coast estate in nearby Woodmere called Foxhall. Instead it was developed with 30 houses. There were 179,000,000 Americans. "Ben-Hur" won the Oscar for Best Picture. In May of that year, Gary Powers' U-2 spy plane was shot down, "The Fantasticks" began its 42 year run at the Sullivan Street Playhouse, the FDA approved an oral contraceptive, Mossad agents abducted Adolf Eichman in Buenos Aires, returning him to Israel for trial, and Sputnik was launched into orbit by the

Soviet Union. Domino's Pizza was founded, and Harper Lee published "To Kill a Mockingbird."

In July of 1960 Ceylon elected Mrs. Sirimavo Bandaranaike as Prime Minister, the world's first woman elected head of government. Rafer Johnson starred in the decathalon in the summer Olympics in Rome, and Cassius Clay won the gold medal in the light heavyweight boxing division. In September, Hurricane Donna lashed the Eastern seaboard and killed 50 people.

That fall, Nikita Kruschez pounded his shoe on a table at the U.N. to protest discussion of Soviet policies in eastern Europe. "The Flintstones" premiered on ABC ("Yabba dabba dabba dabba doo!"), and Richard Nixon and John F. Kennedy appeared in the first televised presidential debate.

My parents watched it in a store window on Madison Avenue after leaving an A. A. meeting in New York.

The great tragedy of the year in my eight year-old world view was the Pirate's defeat of the Yankees in the seventh game of the World Series, despite being heavily outscored over the seven games. Kennedy defeated Nixon in a close election, and "Peter Pan" and "The Wizard of Oz" returned to TV.

If I have only middling memories of early teachers (kindergarten was Miss Hatcher, known, inevitably as "The Hatchet"; second grade was a Dutch woman with a moustache named Miss Van Dort; and third grade a genteel Scots widow named Mrs. Thompson, who always appeared on the verge of fainting thanks to the brutish behavior with which she was confronted), there was no ambiguity of feeling between Miss Anna Smith, our fourth grade teacher, and me. She disliked me from the start, and the sentiment was mutual.

Miss Smith was an elderly, craggy-faced, Ulster woman, who in those pre-politically correct days minced no words in her dislike of Catholics (I would estimate that there were twenty or so in the student body in those days; the number of Jewish students was about ten, and that was the Rainbow of diversity, such as it was), and I was occasionally late to school on account of sometimes serving as an altar boy at early Mass at St. Joachim's in Cedarhurst. She shrewdly sized me up as a slacker, detaining me from several sporting event so as to redo my work. Miss Smith was an idiosyncratic instructor in the standard curriculum but an ardent advocate of nudism in the home, of bra-less blouses in the workplace, and her annual trip to the bare-bosomed statuary of the Egyptian Wing of the Metropolitan Museum of Art was an occasion of great glee to her students.

And yet Miss Smith principally lives on in my memory for the glorious incident that occurred on the afternoon of Hallowe'en in 1961. As she turned in her chair to look in a mirror that stood on a book shelf nearby so that she could apply rouge and lipstick, a breeze rose through an open window, the mirror tottered and fell with a resounding smash, and a truly gratifying spread of shattered shards of glass scattered around the floor. As decorum yielded to a tsunami of hysteria on the students' side of the classroom, Miss Smith gamely faced us, smiled and said, "Seven years of bad luck."

1961 was the year Dwight Eisenhower warned against the military-industrial complex in his farewell speech, JFK electrified the nation in his Inaugural: "Ask not what your country can do for you, but what you can do for your country." President Kennedy established the Peace Corps that April. In the same month the Russian Yuri Gagarin orbited the earth once, becoming the first human in space. Later in April the Bay of Pigs invasion failed miserably.

In May Alan Shepard became the first American in space in the Mecrury program. In June Rudolf Nureyev defected from Russia while in Paris with the Kirov Ballet. On another cultural note, Six Flags opened in Texas the next month. In early October Roger Maris broke Babe Ruth's home run record with his 61st, my hero Mickey Mantle trailing with 54 after an injury-plagued season.

Baseball was my first athletic obsession, and I spent endless hours recreating Yankee games by throwing a tennis ball against the brick façade of our house at 50 Cedarhurst Avenue. The batting order at that time was Bobby Richardson, second base, leading off; then Tony Kubek, shortstop; then Maris. Mickey Mantle was the clean up hitter, followed by Yogi Berra or, later, Elston Howard. First basemen Moose Skowren batted sixth, left fielder Hector Lopez seventh, Golden-gloved third baseman Clete Boyer eighth and the pitcher ninth, although, since he was so good at opposite field doubles, when Whitey Ford was on the mound that could be quite exciting.

I was the fifth of the six boys in our family, and all the rest were right handed, so, I learned to play the way they did, but I did teach myself to switch hit in an homage to my hero. Like the Mick, I had more power from the left-handed side but a higher batting average from the right. That is, until I encountered my first curve ball.

My games of throwing the tennis balls up against the side of the house (lower for grounders and line drives, higher up against the third floor for extra bases and home runs) were rudely interrupted by mother when she heard the ball connecting with a window pane or by Dad, if he was home, who did not appreciate being awakened from the nap he liked to take in his dressing room.

Then I would retreat to the radio or black and white TV. We got 7 channels: 2 (WCBS), 4 (WNBC), 5 (WNEW), 7 (WABC), 9 (WOR), 11 (WPIX)—the Yankees channel, and finally Channel 13, the educational broadcasting network. I listened to Mel Allen ("Hello there, everybody!"), Red Barber ("Sittin' in the catbird seat," or "They're tearin' up the peapatch.") and the Scooter, retired shortstop Phil Rizzuto ("Holy Cow!") narrate the play-by-play with their signature expressions. The Scooter also made rueful commentary on current events, such as when the announcement of Pope John XXIII's death came on the air during a game: "Gee, that puts something of a damper even on a Yankee's win."

The Mickey Mouse Club, Davy Crockett, The Swamp Fox, Red Skelton, and The Million Dollar

Movie were all highly rated programs in our house as well.

Summers were idyllic. We played baseball in the backyard or on the golf course, and I began a life-long love affair with tennis. Golf was a more frustrating pursuit, but the beauty of the seven water holes on the Hunt Club links with its gentle breezes and teeming bird life was a constant source of beauty and peace. David Rutter and I walked the protective dike on the west bank of Crooked Creek that ran from behind his house at the Cedarhurst Yacht Club all the way back to The Causeway. It was filled in those days with turtles, snakes, herons, egret, cormorant, swans and other bird life. At night the fireflies would light up our backyards as we played ball in the waning light, and as summer lengthened the sound of the cicadas rose.

Then there was the ocean ten minutes away, the beautiful white sands and dunes of Atlantic Beach. Most days we got there on the bus driven by Otis, a gentle giant in his dark glasses and driver's cap, who plied a route from the Lawrence School down Ocean Avenue and ultimately across the Atlantic Beach Bridge. We took swimming and diving lessons from 1956 Olympic and longtime Williams coach Bob Muir—a great, wise and gentle man. As we got older we would body surf and cruise to the other beach clubs nearby, or sometimes crawl under the boardwalk to beneath the Ladies Sunroom where naked sunbathing was rumored to occur; but the spaces between the slats in the boardwalk were too narrow to get a good look.

Later we would cross Reynolds Channel in Bobby Hart's Boston Whaler, drinking beers at night and skinny dipping, or waterskiing under the moonlight into the narrows of Crooked Creek.

We lived in a three story, vaguely Georgian brick house with more than enough bedrooms to sleep six boys, my parents, Mary O'Connell, the cook, and Nanny, the tiny but indomitable Theresa Gately, who in time, after Mary married, would take over the housekeeping and cooking as well. Since my eldest brothers were nine and ten years older they were already away in boarding school and college by the time I remember much, more like uncles than brothers. In those pre-Google days my principal utility to them was as a reference resource to settle sports trivia disputes they entered into in one or another of the village taverns. They would put a dime into the pay phone by the bar, dial CE 9-6877 and ask Theresa to wake me so they could settle the bet they had made. "What did Joe Dimaggio bat in 1941?" When Mother heard about it she was not amused.

The house had a large front hall, a formal dining room, pantry, kitchen and laundry room, a beautifully furnished but seldom used living room, and behind that a sunroom where we boys mostly congregated to rough house or watch TV. Over a blueberry pancake breakfast after church on Sunday mornings, we would fight over the *Daily News* or *Herald Tri*bune "Funnies" (the comics sections) and the sports pages. On week-night evenings Dad would bring the evening papers as well—the *Journal-American, The World Telegram,* and *The Post.*

Our parents were readers and tended to stay by the fire in the little den beside the dining room. Occasionally, however, Mom and Dad would invade the TV porch to watch Kelso run on a Saturday or the Giants play on Sunday afternoons. On Sunday night, we would often eat burgers on a tray there as we watched "Bonanza" or Dad's Eli classmate, Efrem Zimbalist Jr., on "The FBI."

In the fifth grade our class was graced by an extraordinary English teacher. Derek Sutton had read history and been a chorister at Kings College, Cambridge. He had the ability to infuse his students with the excitement of learning—most especially the high points of English history-- and the necessity to express oneself clearly and precisely in speech and writing. He arranged pen pals for us in the UK. He also had a fine tenor voice and gave several exhilarating concerts to the school. At year's end he gave us farewell gifts. Fred Alexandre received "The Moonstone" by Wilkie Collins. Mr. Sutton gave me "The Mayor of Casterbridge." Because he had given it to me I struggled terrifically to read it that summer, and out of that experience began a love affair with Hardy's fiction and poetry that endures to this day. Derek returned to London and eventually became the headmaster of the St. Paul's Cathedral Choir School, in which connection he was televised worldwide supervising his charges during the Royal Wedding of Charles and Diana in 1981. He retired to his native York, still assisting at the Minster, and, with a group of fellow senior choristers, singing Sunday services at outlying parishes throughout Yorkshire. Upon his death he was accorded the honor of being buried in the precincts of York Minster, beneath his favorite stained glass window.

In that year, 1962, two of the high-wire Flying Wallendas were killed when their seven person pyramid collapsed during a performance in Detroit. We watched on a miniscule TV in the assembly hall on February 20th as John Glenn orbited the Earth three times and crashed safely in the ocean after. Wilt Chamberlain scored 100 points in an NBA game. The film of "West Side Story" won the Oscar for Best Picture. Rwanda and Burundi gained Independence. Rachel Carson's "Silent Spring" was published.

A recent Oscar season's award nominee, *My Week with Marilyn*, was a charming movie based on a memoir by Colin Clark (younger son of Sir Kenneth

Clark of *Civilization* fame), and beautifully acted by Kenneth Branagh as Sir Laurence Olivier and Michelle Williams as the eponymous starlet. It brought back memories of seeing *Some Like It Hot* at the Central Theatre in Cedarhurst one Saturday matinee, our sainted Irish Nanny being "in the roars of laughter" at the cross-dressing antics of Tony Curtis and Jack Lemmon, and my younger brother and I laughing along with her. Mother was not quite so amused as we at Nanny's choice of films for a seven and four year old (apparently *Old Yeller* or a Jerry Lewis comedy like *Hole in the Head* would have been more "appropriate"), but no lasting harm was done. I still think Billy Wilder's masterpiece is the funniest movie ever made, and I was in love with Marilyn (aka "Sugar Kowalchuk") ever after.

I mention this because the summer of 1962 was my first, blissful experience of sleepaway camp (Nanny did not accompany me but thoughtfully sent up shoeboxes of brownies and chocolate chip cookies every fortnight). Camp Monadnock was outside of Jaffrey Center, New Hampshire, just across Thorndike Pond from Mount Monadnock, at 3165 feet the most prominent New England mountain peak south of the White Mountains and east of the Berkshires. The word means "mountain that stands alone," and the physical setting was spectacular. At chapel in a stand of pristine birches we would sing:

Here at the foot of Monadnock,
Towering over the plain;
Here at the edge of the waters,
Sing we our glad refrain.

There was swimming, canoeing, sailing, archer rifle range, and nature program. The July 4th counselors' softball game was between Yale and Harvard, and there were almost enough guys from those two colleges on staff to field a complete team (some assistance from Amherst and Williams usually did the trick). We saluted the flag at dawn and sundown, played ping pong on the porch and thumper at the dinner table, sang beer jingles (but drank only "bug juice," a low rent Kool Aid), sucked on Sugar Daddys, rowed to our tent's private campsite on the lake for cookouts once a week, told scary stories around the campfire, contested Indian and Naval War Games, read Edgar Allen Poe by a blazing fire in the Lodge on rainy mornings, and ended the seven week season with a Treasure Hunt that began with the annual appearance of Phineas T. Spalding, a pirate who had lived underneath the Pond for the last 200 years. Future Pulitzer Prize winning cartoonist Jeff MacNelly was an assistant counselor who drew brilliant posters for the Saturday night movie. The season ended with campers' and counselors' Follies that were almost as hilarious as *Some Like It Hot*. As the buses started up to take us back to Boston or New York on closing day, the counselors would sing to the tune of "Bye Bye Baby,"

Bye bye kiddies,

Just remember you're our kiddies,

When you go back to School,...

And we did, often with a catch in our throat.

The absolute highlight of the camp calendar, however, was the Long Camping Trip fortnight (or "LCTs"), when myriad groups went forth to climb or canoe around New England. My first year our gang walked the Long Trail until it crested at Stowe, on top of Mount Mansfield, more than a thousand feet higher than Mount Monadnock, and a good test for a ten year old after walking up and down several other peaks on along the four day trip. It was a Sunday morning when we walked off the mountain, and our counselors let us go into the general store at the bottom to store up on Hershey Bars and M&Ms for the long ride back to camp. I was also interested in checking out how Mickey Mantle and Roger Maris were doing for the Yankees and invested in a Sunday *Herald Tribune*. The headline was huge: **MARILYN MONROE IS DEAD AT 36**.

First love is often painful, they tell us, but all I can say is that it had been a great three years; and I am grateful to Colin Clark's movie for reminding me so happily of my own affair with Marilyn.

In October of 1962 James Meredith registered at the University of Mississippi, accompanied by Federal marshals. The first Bond film, *Dr. No*, was released in October. The Cuban Missile Crisis began on October 14th and was not defused until the Soviets began dismantling their missles in early November. The 1962-3 newspaper strike began in New York City and lasted for 114 days. It was painful since there was so little sports on TV, comparatively speaking, in those days. Eventually a strike-breaking paper was put out out with much reduced copy, and we had to make to do with that and the weekly magazines like *Time, Life* and *Sports Illustrated*.

Leonardo da Vinci's Mona Lisa was exhibited in the US for the first time at the National Gallery in January of 1963. Patsy Cline was killed in a plane crash in March. *Lawrence of Arabia* was shown on a giant screen on Broadway and won the Oscar for Best Picture. It went on forever, and the myth of there being surreptitious Coca Cola ads built into the desert scenes was highly credible to my best friend, Lars Potter, and me. On August 28, 1963 Martin Luther King delivered his "I Have a Dream" speech on the steps of the Lincoln Memorial to a crowd of over 250,000 people.

One Friday afternoon that November we walked home from a touch football game on the golf course (school let out at noon on Fridays so we could have our doctors' and dental appointments), and learned that President Kennedy had been shot. John

Jankosky, my mother's contractor, was redoing the television room, his transistor radio blaring, when I came in. He was a large, florid man, bent over with grief, choking back tears.

(Today few remember that Aldous Huxley and C.S. Lewis died the same day.)

Two days later we were sitting at John Carr's house watching the television with his father, Rufus, when Lee Harvey Oswald was led from prison and Jack Ruby, a night club owner with reputed mob ties, jumped out from the crowd and shot him.

But the year ended more happily as The Beatles released "I Want to Hold Your Hand," and "I Saw Her Standing There," on the day after Christmas, and Beatlemania became global.

There were other fine teachers at the School as we were promoted to the Senior Department. DeeDee Baker came out of retirement to teach us Latin with exemplary clarity in our seventh-grade year. Her reading of "A Christmas Carol" to the class was unforgettable. I also never forgot her telling us she believed that pet dogs and cats had souls, although years later, in her second career as a priest of the Episcopal Church, she told me she did not remember that. Mr. Wilson made us memorize all of New York State's sixty-something counties and innumerable dates in the Revolutionary and Civil Wars. Miss Littlefield taught music for over twenty years and produced one or another of the Gilbert and Sullivan operettas each spring. When the class got carried away she would lay her head on the piano keyboard and hit high C until order was restored, but her good humor never gave out completely, and she took a train into town every week to attend church services and teach Sunday school.

Mr. Clark guided us through the mysteries of early algebra, often exclaiming, "Don't just stand there like mashed potatoes and beefsteak." He never quite could make an experiment work in the often smoke-filled science lab, confounded us with his "mystery ball" on the mound and, in his frequent visits to their apartment in the converted campus garage, was a daily example of utter devotion to his invalid wife.

In 1964 Barry Goldwater won the Republican nomination for president, beating out Senator Margaret Chase Smith, the first woman to run for president, Nelson Rockefeller and Pennsylvania

Governor William Scranton. Surgeon General Luther Terry reported that smoking *may* be hazardous to health. *Meet the Beatles* was released in January. The next month the Fab Four arrived in America and appeared on the Ed Sullivan show, seen by 73 million viewers. *Hello Dolly* opened on Broadway. Cassius Clay beat Sonny Liston in Miami to become heavyweight champion. The first Mustang rolled off the line at the Ford Motor Company. Richard Burton and Elizabeth Taylor married for the first time. Merv Griffin's *Jeopardy* debuted on NBC. The Polo Grounds, hallowed temple of the baseball and football Giants and later the Mets and Titans (the original name of the Jets), was demolished. Sidney Poitier was the first African-American to win the Oscar for best actor in *Lilies of the Field.* The World's Fair opened in New York.

Terence Conran opened his first store on London's Fulham Road. 12 young men in New York burned their draft cards. Nelson Mandela was sentenced to life imprisonment on Robben Island. Ken Keysey and his Merry Pranksters set off on Further (their bus) to spread the gospel of LSD. Jim Bunning pitched a perfect game for the Phillies, the first since 1880 in the National League. Three civil rights workers, Michael Schwerner, Andrew Goodman, and James Chaney were murdered near Philadelphia, Mississippi by local Klansmen and a deputy sheriff. On July 2nd Lyndon Johnson signed the Civil Rights Act of 1964 into law.

Mary Poppins, My Fair Lady and *Goldfinger* premiered. In October Nikita Kruschev was deposed in the Soviet Union, succeeded by Leonid

Brezhnev and Alexi Kosygin. The Verrazano-Narrows Bridge, the world's longest suspension bridge at the time, opened. 800 were arrested at a Berkeley Free Speech protest. Dr. Martin Luther King won the Nobel peace Prize. And Rudy Gernreich's monokini toples swimsuit was featured in *Look*.

There were several other colorful figures at the Lawrence School. Frank Behne, the gravel-voiced superintendent, taught shop as he chain-smoked in the basement and regaled us with stories of General Pershing's expedition into Mexico in search of Pancho Villa. Fred and Nora Martens ran the kitchen and stoically produced meals that after the privations of boarding school and college one remembers as having been pretty good, none more so than the treat of outdoor cook-outs on fair fall and spring days, when the smell of hamburgers on the grill would waft through open classroom windows and end all hope of concentrating on the subject at hand. They were assisted by a fellow German named Emmie, who spoke almost no English, and when asked what was for lunch would always answer exuberantly, "Pumpkin Pie!" a dish that was never served. Emmie had lost her husband in World War II, and set a place for him at dinner every night in her rented room.

Our food at home, by contrast, was delicious and beautifully served as mother presided over her table with bell in hand. Roast chicken, lamb, pot roast and a variety of fish on Fridays, including soul amandine, baked clams, and cream of tuna with sliced hard-boiled eggs peering out of it like fish eyes. For special occasions there might be squab or crown roast. Nanny's and Mary's popovers (or, occasionally, pop unders) were highly anticipated as were the cakes, pies, ice creams and souffles they so lovingly prepared.

Mother was gregarious and completely devoted to family. Both of her sisters had moved to Lawrence after the War, so we had sixteen first cousins close by. My father suffered from bi-polar disorder. When depressed, he slept for sixteen hours a day and sometimes could not even bear to get out of his pajamas to dress for dinner. On one of his highs, on the other hand, he would be up at five, into his Wall Street firm early and, after lunch at the Squadron A Club in the Biltmore Hotel, to his family real estate office in the Lincoln Building. He would plan trips, attend multiple AA meetings, bringing his comrades from there home for weekends, and filling the house with chatter and laughter. He was handsome, athletic, charismatic and funny; but even in those very good times I remember noticing the plumes of cigarette smoke rising from both ends of the dining table. Mother smoked three packs of Marlboros a day and Dad four packs of the non-filtered Chesterfields. As the years went on their coughing worsened.

So long as Dad was well the house was wide open. Family and friends were always welcome to drop in for a drink or dinner, or to stay the night over. In summer, we for the most part lived on the airy screen porch in the back of the house, looking out over the terrace, back lawn and large apple tree at the back of the property. I can still remember the taste of the slightly warming milk Mary would put out in a silver pitcher half an hour before dinner was served.

Our bedrooms had fans in the summer (although eventually Mom and Dad acquired an air conditioner). There were frogs, garter snakes, and lots of rabbits in the field adjacent to our house. Behind us was an abandoned stable where you could still find a horse shoe or two. The attics on the third floor were filled with curiosities, and one had a hidden room where I set up a private club.

I can remember the cry of the crickets, the many birds, the smell of mint growing in the laundry pen beside the garage, the acrid smell of the vinegar Nanny applied to her County Roscommon skin to ward of the burn of the beach sun, the taste of her bacon sandwiches as we ate them on the sand, the musty air of the attics, the flowers blooming in the garden Mother tended, the silver and furniture polish, the honey suckle vines blooming in the heat of summer, the beetles beneath the curb stones in the driveway, and the two new cherry trees blooming in the front yard.

I can remember the wind blowing across the 7th fairway as Dad redeemed an ill-considered January promise to take me camping on the golf course one June evening. With great hilarity Mother helped us load up the station wagon and escorted us to the tent-pitching site. Under the moonlight I asked if he liked sleeping outside, and he told me with complete conviction he would rather sleep like this than anywhere else. In the morning I declined his offer to go to the country club for a "really good" breakfast and enjoyed putting my slice of bread on a stick to toast above the fire. When we got home I followed my father up the stairs and into the master bedroom where he plunked himself down beside Mother eating breakfast in bed off her tray and groaned, "God, this is the most comfortable thing I have ever felt in my life."

Lawrence School's smaller size made competing against Buckley and Greenvale in football, basketball and baseball ever challenging, but we held our own. We looked forward to sports all day. I am angered when I read of large doses of Ritalin being prescribed for "hyperactive" boys in schools—especially inner city schools—today. A far better medicine would be ninety minutes of strenuous exercise under the guidance of a competent coach from whom young men could learn the value of working together as a team for a goal greater than oneself. *Mens sana in corpore sano.*

We were all athletes: Dad a fine horseman, tennis letter winner at Yale and several time Club champion; Mom a good golfer; Phil nationally ranked in squash and a leading tennis player as well; Schuyler a triple threat in football, hockey and baseball, who went on to be called " the poor man's Roger Staubach" in the Washington *Post* when he quarterbacked the Georgetown team back into competitive football; Kevin a fine squash and racquets champion; Pierce in many ways the best coordinated, a squash and skiing wonder; and Peter a squash champion and court tennis player. But in those days it was most often touch football on the sidelawn and hitting pop flies up into the darkening summer sky, water polo at the beach, and tennis in the sunset's lingering light.

Some summers I visited my cousins in Urbana, Ohio and ate peppermint ice cream with butterscotch sauce after typing lessons at summer school and swimming in the local pool. I announced Little League baseball games at the small stadium and sang along with songs John and Chip McCarty played on the piano. Then we would drive far north to Wyquewetonsing next to Harbor Springs on the upper peninsula and water ski on Lake Michigan. I remember watching NBC's *Game of the Week* at the resort's only TV, at the one hotel, Aunt Barbara baking delicious bread, playing ping pong at the old-fashioned Casino and softball against the inmates at the local penitentiary. One day Uncle Buddy, who had been shot down twice behind enemy lines in Europe during the war, took me up in his plane to fly over the the awe-inspiring Macinack Straits.

Realizing my younger brother Peter would eventually be left alone at home, my father brought a wonderful flat-coated retriever named Paget for him to keep company with, and Peter sweetly shared the joy of dog ownership and many adventures and misadventures with me.

LBJ proclaimed "The Great Society" early in 1965. Shortly thereafter, Sir Winston Churchill died at 91, and his State Funeral exceeded all others in pomp and ceremony. Henry Luce chartered an airplane and outfitted it with dark rooms so that his *Life* photographers would have the scoop on other magazines.

In March *The Sound of Music* premiered at the Rivoli Theatre. 5 days later, on March 7th, some 200 Alabama state troopers attacked 525 civil rights demonstraters in Selma as they marched to the state capital in Montgomery. In late March funeral services were held for Violet Liuzzo, who was shot dead by 4 Klansmen as she drove marchers back to Klansmen after the civil rights march.

On May 9th Vladimir Horowitz returned to the stage after a 12 year absence to perform a triumphant concert at Carnegie Hall. In July Bob Dylan "went electric" at the Newport Folk Festival. The Beatles "HELP" premiered in theatres. In August the Watts riots began in LA. Casey Stengel announced his retirement from the Amazin' Mets after 55 years in baseball.

Pope Paul VI visited the US. (In John Guare's play "House of Blue Leaves" groupies wear their "Paul" buttons from The Beatles recent trip). In October the Saarinen "Gateway Arch" was completed in St. Louis.

In November John Lindsay was elected Mayor of New York, over the insouciant Conservative, William. F. Buckley Jr., and Democrat Abraham Beame.

But before Fun City could begin, on November 9th the Northeast Blackout cut power for over 13 hours. We lit candles at home, tickled our overnight guest Carolyn Carpenter, and relished the reprieve from homework.

In December *A Charlie Brown Christmas* aired for the first time. In January of 1966, Mike Quill and the Transit Workers Union went on strike and Fun City was not so fun for "Mr. Linley" thereafter. Nat King Cole died in February.

The times were changing. In April *Time* magazine asked on its black cover: "Is God Dead?" As our TV tastes became more sophisticated we tuned to "Shindig," "Hullaballoo" and "The Man from U.N.C.L.E.," all the more so when the daughter of Mom's best friend, model Katherine Carpenter, married David McCallum, who played the long-haired Ilya Kuryakin in the series.

In June of 1966, our class graduation coincided with the 75th Anniversary of the founding of the Lawrence School, and we were invited to join the large luncheon that followed Commencement Exercises on the circle lawn in front of the school. Mr. Barber returned for the occasion, and prominent alumni reminisced on their respective eras at the School. *Life* Magazine columnist Loudon Wainwright, also an alumnus, gave the keynote address, at one point remarking he believed he could still find the gap in the hedge where he had used to steer his bicycle onto the school grounds early in the morning.

I was glad to be moving on. The truth was that I was bored to death the last several years at the school and had asked to be sent away in the eighth grade. My father talked me out of it, counseling I might enjoy being a big fish in a small pond rather than being back on the bottom rung of the ladder. He spoke from experience, having been sent off to the then still new Portsmouth Priory in the seventh grade in the early 1930s. So I stayed on, enjoyed my family and friends, editing the school newspaper, playing sports, early mornings by the fire reading the paper with my Dad, walking Paget to the village after school to buy baseball cards, and the first horribly awkward parties with girls, where virginal kisses playing Spin the Bottle tended to taste of potato chips and M&Ms. I read and wrote a favorable review of *The Green Berets* that year, and, not long after, Katherine Carpenter's brother George, my old camp counselor, left Yale suddenly, signed up with the Marines and was shipped off to Viet Nam.

I remember the joy of riding bikes to school, pedaling through the back lanes of Lawrence, Cedarhurst, Woodsburgh, Woodmere, and Hewlett

Bay Park, chattering and laughing with one's companions, while smelling the fallen leaves in fall or the intermingled fragrances of lilac, azalea, blossoming fruit trees and freshly mown grass in spring. But the actual days in class became endless. I was sure something more exciting lay beyond the perimeter or our little world, and if boarding school was the way to get there, my feeling was: bring it on.

II. Fall-- 1966

1.

We weren't due at Portsmouth until 6 PM my first day that September, but Mother was an early bird and got me there by noon. When we got to St. Bede's she knocked on the housemaster's door, and a mellifluous voice bellowed, "COME." I opened the door and saw a middle-aged man in the Benedictine black habit with precisely parted but thinning grey hair seated at his desk. He was holding a black lamb and feeding it milk from a baby bottle.

"Come in, dear boy. Why hello Joan, so good to see you."

We sat on the sofa, as Father Hilary continued to feed the lamb.

"Very rarely a ewe will have triplets, and then there's no room at the inn, so we have to feed the odd man out. It's even rarer that one of them be black. His name is Formosa. Here, why don't you feed him? I'll look for your room assignment." He plopped Formosa on my lap and gave me the bottle before I could protest. After a minute he looked over and said firmly, "Jamie, one must support the head while feeding."

I did as I was told as he consulted his list. "Ah yes, just as I thought. Murray. Marvelous!"

Father Hilary—sun-tanned at the end of summer and surprisingly strong, carried my bags to my room and gave me a quick tour of the surroundings. Saint Bede's was the first piece of modern architecture to be built on a campus that had previously been burdened with stolid neo-Gothic red brick buildings, the first stage of a grand design that had happily been halted by the Depression. St. Bede's was made of redwood and fieldstone with large plate glass windows surrounding an inner courtyard that suggested a contemporary cloister. Father Hilary said something that sailed way over my head about it being a "Fifties restatement of International Style," and that his friend George Nakashima had designed the wonderfully abstract but tree-like wooden furniture. I just knew I liked the sense of openness and the abundance of natural light in the building.

Father Hilary assured me that my roommate and I would get along well. "He's just come back from Europe," he exclaimed, as if that assured our compatability. I imagined a scholarly, continental type. When Tommy Murray arrived from Washington that evening he was wearing tight blue jeans, engineer boots, a green suede jacket with a button pinned to its lapel that read, "Let's Legalize Pot," Carnaby Street cufflinks with a Peter Max design, and had longer, bushier dark brown hair than anyone else I had observed in the dining hall at supper. In 1966 that meant that it just about covered his shirt collar.

"Hi," I said, extending my hand.

"Scooby doo," he answered, flicking his hair, and turned away. It was the last thing I heard him say until the Headmaster sent him for a haircut the next morning, after which he ranted and raved about how much he hated schools and barbers. But that night, after lights were out, he decided it was a good time to converse.

"My father took Jackie Kennedy to see the bulls run in Pamplona last summer."

"Really?"

"Yeah. Then he and I went to Morocco and England."

"That sounds neat."

"Yeah, neat," he echoed snidely. "And my uncle runs the biggest bank on the West Coast."

"Oh."

"Who's famous in your family?"

"Uh, no one."

"Hm."

Tommy was unimpressed. In due course I learned that his family were Californians who had operated newspapers for generations. His mother had rebelled and set up shop in Georgetown, where she was active in population control and global family planning programs. His father was head of *Time* magazine's Madrid bureau.

I had little to contribute to such staggering sophistication, so after a while Tommy stopped making small talk and began drumming Wilson Pickett's "Wait Till the Midnight Hour" on the room's cinder block wall as he sang along, off key. In time I discouraged this practice by lobbing some of my heavier textbooks across the room toward his knuckles, but in those early days I was still intimidated by him and everything else about Portsmouth.

I remember every detail about the first time I entered the church at Portsmouth Abbey, from the flagstone floor to the sculpted redwood beams, to the spun-gold wires that ran from the cross above the altar all the way up to the chapel's rafters. It was patterned on the sixth century Church of San Vitale in Ravenna, commissioned by the Emperor Justinian in Saint Benedict's lifetime.

Inside there was a sense of soaring verticality as one looked up at the great, laminated birch arches that supported the chapel tower. In January wind roared off the water and buffeted the building so that the chapel creaked and shuddered like an old ship as she tried to turn into an increasingly hostile storm.

The first time I went to Sunday Mass there the monks filed by, cowled and vested, older men of course, and yet by all appearances having worn their years lightly. When you're young everyone seems old. When you reach middle age, however, you immediately search out any sign of youth in even the most ancient. Soon they had passed by, bowed toward the altar and seated themselves in their stalls in the retrochoir.

> *In nomine Patris et Filii et Spiritus sancti.*
> *Amen.*

The monastic community and congregation made the sign of the cross, and the Mass began with the sonorous sounds and rising and falling tones of Gregorian chant. Incense wafted around the altar and up toward the roof. As it rose it refracted in the sunlight streaming through the stained-glass windows, and smoke and light swirled in a steadily ascending cloud.

> *Confiteor*
> *Deo omnipotenti*

*Et vobis, fratres, quia peccavi nimis
Cogitatione, verbo, opere et omissione*

Mea culpa, mea culpa, mea maxima culpa....

Through my *own* fault.

We went through all the new school year rituals, the orientation meetings, the endless lists of very rigid rules and nearly non-existent privileges. Then classes began and with them crushing homework assignments and endless study halls, the hours of the day crammed with obligations from before dawn until ten at night. Father Hilary's solicitude was not shared by his chief prefect, a sadistic all-state football tackle, who beat me up whenever the opportunity presented itself. Among other duties he assigned me was to help in the delegation that carried him up to the early morning Tuesday Mass at 6 AM. A group of flunkies would heave and strain under the half-dressed prefect, still asleep in his bed. At the chapel steps we put on his jacket, tie and shoes, led him to his pew and propped him up. After Mass we woke him for breakfast.

In those days everyone else seemed to know the routine and I was constantly struggling to figure it out. I always seemed to be spilling cereal on my shirt or walking around with my tie sticking out of my open fly. My mother had generously bought me a wardrobe of khaki trousers and button-down shirts, regimental ties and a couple of sports jackets at Brooks Brothers the week before I came to Portsmouth. But the other guys all looked comfortable in their clothes, whereas I felt awkward in mine and out of place in general.

In the junior common room of St. Bede's I got to know some of my classmates. Bacardi was a scrawny and sarcastic Cuban, Raho a tough, stocky Greek-Italian, and Branson a black Boys' Club Boy of the Year scholarship winner from Columbus, Ohio. They lounged around the common room, discussing the merits of The Animals' "House of the Rising Sun" versus The Kingsmen's "Louie Louie" or the Dixie Cups "Chapel of Love" which Branson endlessly mimicked in falsetto.

Fierce literary argument also raged. Which was the coolest—Green Hornet, Metamorpho, or Spiderman?

At one point I asked, "Has anyone read "The Caine Mutiny?"

"What kind of comic is that?"

"It was our summer reading assignment," I replied wanly, and from the way everyone else's eyes glazed over I could tell I had betrayed myself as the uncoolest of the uncool.

2.

My iniquities were like a snowball growing in size as it rolls.

(The Confessions of Saint Augustine)

After the initial hurricane of hyper-scheduled weeks the first sliver of semi-free time appeared. Classes were held on Saturday mornings, of course, but Portsmouth had neglected to devise a fitting form of torture for every Saturday afternoon. If the varsity football team was playing at home we were strongly encouraged to attend; if they were away we were encouraged slightly less enthusiastically (lest the school have to bear the cost of transporting too many students by bus). I had considered going to the away game but decided instead to walk into the village. Tommy Murray had never considered going to the game and was also walking into the village. He had made friends with Porter Carroll, an ectomorphic inhabitant of the room next to ours in St. Bede's. I played on the junior varsity football team with Carroll but didn't know him well. He was tall, sandy-haired, and sunburned, came from Miami, had started at Portsmouth a year earlier in its 8th grade, and was deeply interested in the mechanics of automobile engines. This did not at first blush suggest that he and Tommy would have much to talk about, but Tommy recruited him anyway because Porter knew a short cut to the village that ran through adjoining farmland rather than the long way around on public roads.

Porter proved to be a friendly and knowledgeable, if often monosyllabic, guide as he led us over the remains of 300 year-old stone walls and 19th century lanes. His favorite phrase was *"Tranquilo,"* which he assured us everything was the several times Tommy asked him if we were lost. It took us an hour or so to make the three-mile hike. It was a clear autumn day, and the leaves were just beginning to turn. The stone walls painstakingly constructed from cleared fields by generations of Rhode Island farmers were perfectly piled and joined. A herd of Jerseys huddled at one end of a sloppy field.

The village was a disappointment when we got there. Portsmouth had a small supermarket hard by the American Legion headquarters, a dry cleaner, a bakery and a liquor store. I volunteered to give the liquor store a try and was promptly thrown out by the grizzled owner. So we ordered frappes at the soda fountain of the pharmacy, bought orange juice, sodas and fruit at the supermarket and stopped off at the bakery to purchase a large cheesecake. While Tommy was trying to decide whether to go with the strawberry or plain topping, I noticed Porter eyeing another part of the display window.

"I'll have a can of the Freon, please."
He stuttered slightly, and the shopkeeper looked at him suspiciously.

"What do you want that for?"
Porter looked at him innocently.

"We just want to spray it on our coke bottles before we drink them. They don't let us use refrigerators at school."

"OK," the shopkeeper relented, "But be careful. Some kids get in trouble with these."

She pointed to the illustration on the box, which showed a martini glass being frosted by the spray.

As we lugged our loot back across the fields Tommy turned to Porter and demanded,

> "What did you buy that Freon shit for?"
>
> "Wait a couple of minutes and I'll show you."

A couple of hundred yards up we followed Porter into an empty pasture beside a creek, surrounded by stone walls. Porter reached into his shopping bag and pulled out a box of Baggies.

> "What's that?" I asked.
>
> "You ever smoke grass?"

I wasn't sure what he meant, but the indicated answer was clearly yes, so I nodded.

> "You have not."

I had heard of marijuana, but "grass" was new to me. I took it literally, and smoking it did not sound overly exciting. Porter looked at me dubiously though not unkindly.

"Well then, since you've already gotten high, you should be the first to check this stuff out."

He took out the can of Freon, sprayed it into a Baggie until the plastic blew up like a balloon. Then he passed it to me and said, "Go ahead."

"Go ahead and what?"

"Go ahead and inhale it. I'm doing you a huge favor."

"What's it supposed to do?"

"It's like laughing gas. It makes you high."

"How do you know?"

"I re-read about it in *Newsweek* last week. It's become an epidemic among high school retards like us. Now are you going to try or are you chicken?"

This was twenty years before just saying no. The stuff might kill me, but I was damned if I was going to be called a chicken.

In those days I was a fat five feet, four inches with a semi-crew cut to boot. I didn't exactly look like Abbie Hoffman, but I took a deep breath of the stuff, and there was an incredible, instantaneous warm rush to my head. I began to talk but all my words came out three octaves below my normal voice. After another couple of seconds I got dizzy and passed out. When I came to a few seconds later

Tommy and Porter were looking fearfully at me stretched out on the meadow-muffined ground.

They needn't have been concerned. The only thing I was worried about was getting another hit of Freon. Porter and Tommy began inhaling the stuff with a vengeance and were soon staggering all around the field. "*Tranquilo*," Porter said in a stoned voice. "Cool as the breeze," Tommy responded happily. The two of them discovered their mutual love of the Rolling Stones and were soon singing, "I can't get no…*Satisfaction*," ad nauseam. A couple of cows sauntered up to the edge of the adjacent pasture and regarded us from the other side of the stone wall. Tommy made a half-hearted attempt to turn them on as well, and they broke back deeper into the field.

We spent the better part of the afternoon there, trading off hits, before the can gave out. We were all pretty wasted, and I was lying face down in the pasture trying not to blow lunch when one of the monks, Father Andrew, looked quizzically at us as he drove past in his tractor. Porter thought he might report us, so we started moving again. As it was, we were almost late for supper, which would have meant being put on bounds. But we had already promised each other we'd go back into Aquidneck the next weekend and buy every can of Freon we could find. That is, until we got to the dinner table, and Father Hilary remarked drily, "Customarily people clean up before going out to dinner on Saturday night. You'd best follow that practice henceforth, whatever mischief it was you three were up to in the fields this afternoon."

He spoke absolutely deadpan, but there was a hint of merriment flashing in his eyes.

Bill Crimmins was a stylish lay master in his late 30s, who taught ancient history and coached our junior varsity football team. Crimmins had a pair of navy-blue Camaros and enjoyed racing whichever of them he was piloting down the long School driveway.

Sports were primitive at Portsmouth in those days. We practiced football on a severely sloping sheep meadow and basketball in the ancient carriage house of the original estate. Lad, Father Hilary's ancient sheep dog, would occasionally run loose and come down to herd us up into a circle. At the end of an undistinguished season Crimmins threw a party for us at his spacious house on Indian Avenue overlooking the Sakonnet River in Middletown. Students loved him for the generosity of his spirit and his slightly mad nature. Over his desk in his office hung a quotation from *Love's Labours Lost*:

> *There is a gift I have, simple, simple:*
> *A foolish extravagant spirit full of forms,*
> *Figures, shares, objects, ideas,*
> *Apprehensions, motions, revolutions,*
> *These are begot in the ventricle of memory,*
> *And delivered upon the mellowing of occasion*
> *But the gift is good in those whom it is acute*
> *And I am thankful for it.*

Father Hilary had known and loved him since Mr. Crimmins was a boy at Portsmouth, but he didn't hesitate to criticize what he saw as his faults. "Crimmins is the most personally generous man I've ever known, but he has this Irish sense of time, and Life just doesn't work that way."

But Crimmins was crazy like a fox, and often figured out what we were thinking before we had put it into words ourselves.

In November of 1966 the River Arno flood devastated Florence, and Ronald Reagan was elected governor of California.

The week before the all too brief Thanksgiving Weekend, Father Hilary took me aside and asked me to invite Porter home for the holiday. We only got thirty hours off, and Porter couldn't get to his family in Miami and back in that time. We were not yet close friends, and yet when Hilary asked I didn't give calling my mother for permission to bring him a second thought.

The train ride down to New York was crowded with students playing guitars and smoking. Once we got into Penn Station we went to the old Madison Square Garden on 49th Street to see the Rangers get shellacked by Montreal, despite Louie Fontinato back checking Maurice "The Rocket" Richard over the sideboards and into the seats. Then we went downtown to the Village and heard Jim Kweskin and The Jug Band play the Village Gate. Later on we caught the last set at the Blue Note, Danny Kalb singing "Roberta" with The Blues Project. Along the way we drank our share of beers, which back in the days of an eighteen year-old drinking age was not too difficult for fifteen year olds. We also scored some pot from a dealer on Thompson Street that turned out to be almost entirely stalks and seeds and made us cough so hard we choked, although we maintained stoutly to each other that we felt high.

By the time we got back to Long Island we were trashed, and my mother had to wake us at noon. We watched football, ate an outrageous meal, and around four o'clock went back down to Penn Station to get on the train to Providence. But in those few hours of frenzied freedom, however inarticulately, friendship had been forged.

The point of coming back so early from Thanksgiving was to start preparing for the end-of-term exams. I was not looking forward to them. My Latin teacher, Father Julian, had summed up my first marking period performance objectively when he wrote, "Only the occasional yawn would reassure me that he had not fallen asleep altogether."

In December the Yule Log on WPIX debuted.

Among those who died in 1966 were the poet Frank O'Hara, Mississippi John Hurt and Walt Disney.

But our journey was just beginning.

III. 1967

1.

Winters were colder then.

The northwest wind whipped out of the arctic tundra, ripped down Hudson's Bay, gained ferocity from the frigid air at the top of the White Mountain range and raged into the region around Rhode Island from November until mid-April, spraying sheets of icy flame and frozen fire.

On any given night Tommy, Porter, and I were out in such weather walking by the water, or, in winter, out onto the ice of the Bay, when we should have been studying or sleeping or saying our prayers. We would smoke, talk, and watch the night sky, the wind battering our bodies, trying to make sense of our situation in a school run by Benedictine monks with a perspective fourteen centuries long. It was the most painful, hilarious and confusing four years of my life, leaving me with the feeling of being fractured into depression, laughter, and futility for decades after.

What was it about that time and place? Weather played its part. The school, too, was hard. And the times were tumultuous. Wonderful times to grow up in if you were a misfit. Our teachers— Father Andrew, Mr. Crimmins, Father Ambrose, and all the others—were an eccentric, brilliant, sometimes saintly, but even more often
strange, assembly. But of all of them Father Hilary was the most important, managing to be both an inspiration and a mystery. He set his expectations high for himself and for others. We failed to meet them then much of the time, and sometimes he fell

short as well. Yet it was the force of his example that has stayed with me like no other. What he chose to do with his life was far too radical a profession for an adolescent to apprehend, even in what we liked to think was the original radical decade.

But let's be clear about one thing: We made our own beds, at the end of the Sixties.

2.

Portsmouth Priory had been founded by the same man who, in his first career as deacon in the Episcopal Church, had started St. George's's School in nearby Middletown, on the other side of Aquidneck Island, near Newport. John Byron Diman was of an old Bristol family, who may, he thought, have once been slave holders in that well documented slaving port. He was a *magna cum laude* alumnus of Brown, who had in middle age begun to read Cardinal Newman. One night he suffered an attack of appendicitis and almost gave his spinster sister a heart attack in her turn when he asked her to summon a Roman Catholic priest. The cat was then out of the bag, and Diman not only converted to the Catholic Church but also entered Downside, a monastery in the west of England. The Abbot of Downside, however, gave Diman a good looking over, and sent him right back to America to start a Catholic school. Now known as Father Hugh, he found a property near to St.George's, and Portsmouth began. Father Hugh was a Yankee patrician who combined a love of learning with a radiant sympathy for others that attracted monks and students alike to his side. Despite early vicissitudes, Portsmouth soon flourished.

The school was still young when Father Hilary came to it, part of a second wave of monks. Hilary Martin was tall and well-built, with legs like young oak trees, a ruddy complexion and a honeyed yet authoritative voice. To assure a steady supply of food for the boys during World War II, Hilary, still in his first years in the monastery, had used some family funds to start Portsmouth's farm. In consequence he was called "The Good Shepherd" behind his back. It was a nickname he gently disdained and secretly enjoyed.

One morning that first winter I knocked on his door sick with a stomach flu, and, although he was preparing for a class, Father Hilary insisted on walking me down to the Infirmary. He was as kind and generous-spirited then as anyone I have ever known, and I began to wonder how he could have chosen the path he had. What was it, really, that would lead one to such a life?

At the beginning of each term Father Hilary was relaxed, and his mood was mellow. He asked each class in for Tea during evening study hall. He served french pastries and led conversations about politics, literature and the arts. Father Hilary came from San Jose in northern California and had known members of Tommy Murray's family when he was young. When his grandfather had died before his time, Hilary's father had gone to work sweeping the floors of a trading firm. He rose through its ranks until he ran it. "We had a very pleasant life," Father Hilary used to say, recalling croquet matches with his father after Sunday lunch and trips to San Francisco to see the Seals play in the Pacific Coast League. But it was his mother's example that he mentioned most often. She had given their cook standing instructions that no one—friend, tradesman, gardeners or hobos-- was to come away from their house unfed. "When I started the Farm here her words were ringing in my mind."

Father Hilary had come East to go to M.I.T. "I enjoyed college so much," he liked to say, "I stayed for six years." He had become an architect, a member of the faculty at "Tech," and an urban planner in Washington during the New Deal. He had come to the monastery in his thirties, and, however hard he may have tried to escape it, a sense of worldliness always remained with him. How many monk's cells had an original Picasso hanging in them, even if, as he claimed, he had picked it up in Paris for thirty bucks? And for someone who had taken vows of stability, "conversion of morals" and obedience, he had an often ribald sense of humor and was something of a rebel at heart. He was not above raising his pained eyes to high heaven as Father Leo, the headmaster, nattered on to the students from the High Table after lunch on the need to maintain six inches of space between you and your partner at that evening's dance.

But Father Hilary took civilizing us very seriously. At his Teas he played Beethoven or Bruckner, cooked scrambled eggs with truffles and discussed pre-Raphaelite painting, baroque architecture, shepherding and the Sitwells. He prided himself on having cast his first vote for president for Norman Thomas. Often, I wasn't sure of what the hell he was talking about.

And yet Father Hilary had another side to his personality as well. He ran Saint Bede's as if he expected his students to act like adults and to be treated the same. He kept his part of the bargain far better than we kept ours, and the result was that he would eventually become exasperated and angry, his mood ricocheting from enthusiasm to gloom. Then he would shout that he had had enough, withdraw into his room with a choleric cough, and relations would temporarily cease.

This pattern repeated itself every year, but the first year, of course, I thought it was some extraordinary, original event. We were getting along famously until one day he approached me with a worried look on his face and asked why I had not been at morning prayers. "I checked and you weren't in your room, and I had no idea where you could be."

His concern was so genuine that, rather than invent any number of stories about doing field work for Biology or extra running to lose weight, I told him the unvarnished truth. "I'm sorry, Father, but I overslept, and when I heard someone coming I thought it was a prefect, so I jumped into the closet."

Father Hilary grimaced and turned away without a word. That was the last time he spoke to me for two weeks. "That's okay," Bill Crimmins, our history teacher and coach, who had been expelled from the School in his youth, reassured me when I told him about it. "You should take it as a kind of compliment. He didn't speak to me once for two *years*."

But in many ways Father Hilary was one of the least eccentric monks at Portsmouth. Take Father Andrew. He had been a math prodigy and founder of a school in Boston before becoming a monk. He was Portsmouth's registrar, taught several classes, devised the daily schedule for 220 boys without the assistance of a computer, kept the chickens on the Farm, served as cantor at all chapel services and had never been seen asleep. On the contrary, whenever we were out on the campus after lights out, the single biggest challenge was avoiding Father Andrew, who wandered around examining the night sky when he wasn't working through the dawn in his office.

My first brush with him came on the second week of classes that first winter term. I was walking on the upper quadrangle when I heard someone call my name. Flattered that anyone would know who I was, I turned around and saw the wild white mane, soiled black habit and broken-down loafers that were Father Andrew's signatures.

"Good morning, Father."

"Don't give me that good morning crap, aren't you supposed to be in French now?"

Of course I was, and he knew the exact section I should have been in. But it was an advanced section, and after scoring a minus 250 on my first quiz the day before I had received permission from the department chairmen to transfer into a section that was more my speed. I explained this to Andrew, and he nodded.

"Well, then, would you like a pancake?"

It seemed rude to say anything but yes.

"Good."

He reached into his habit and pulled out a soggy brown mass. He proffered it. There was no way out. I took a nibble. He peered at me intently. I decided I'd better take one more bite to be polite. It tasted like a shoe that had been stuck in goose shit for a month or two. Father Andrew stared at me all the more intently.

"Is there something wrong, Father?"

"No, I was just wondering, does that pancake taste all right to you?"

"Yes," I lied, "It tastes fine."

Father Andrew's look turned to one of immense relief. As he wandered off he mumbled over his shoulder, "I'm so glad to hear that. The other night I was out late and got sprayed by a skunk, and I was afraid he might have gotten the pancake too."

When I told him the story Father Hilary roared with laughter and said, "You're merely the latest of his many victims."

Winter descended, and in those days there were no weekends or other relief. I thought this must have been what the Battle of Choisin Reservoir was like. The work was crushing, and three hours of study hall was not nearly enough to complete the math problems, language exercises, science experiments, history essays and English compositions that were assigned daily, let alone the reading homework, which increased exponentially as time went on.

"I hate this place," Tommy grumbled as the workload grew, and even the usually even-tempered Porter Carroll occasionally let out a plaintive, "Oh man."

Perhaps part of my problem was that I was trying to read Tommy's copy of *Evergreen Review* when I might have been better off memorizing the third declension. There was one especially riveting story about how the women of a particular African tribe dug the hole at seeding time but only men could accomplish the actual planting. They walked down the rows pouring seed into the holes and masturbated until they ejaculated on top of the seeds. This process of pre-fertilization, the article argued, was the secret formula that accounted for "the genius of African agriculture."

If you have ever wondered why *Evergreen* is no longer around, it may be that articles like that did not stand up too well to scholarly scrutiny. But they made a strong impression on me, and I seriously considered a career in sub-Saharan agriculture. Of course, when Senor Gumpert, the Spanish master, caught me reading the article in study hall he took a slightly dimmer view of the scholarship than I had. "*Muerta*," he hissed and slapped me across the face.

That same night when I returned to St. Bede's there was a highly unusual note to call home. The news was not good. My old camp counselor, George Carpenter, who had joined the Marines and gone to Vietnam, was dead, blown up by a landmine while on patrol.

After that news focusing on studies was impossible. Instead, we listened to music as often as we could. 1967 was the year of the Jefferson Airplane's "Surrealistic Pillow" album, and The Who's "Tommy."

Father Hilary tried to remain tolerant of the noise level in the common room during the two twenty minute periods each day when records could be played. Often, he raised his eyebrows in amused irony as he walked by. Ten minutes later, however, he was apt to come crashing out of his room and shout, "Shut that thing off right now." It sounded better than Stravinsky to us.

The most interesting thing that happened late that winter term was the night the Prior, an Englishman named Dom Aelred Graham, taught us how to meditate during his weekly chapel talk. Dom Aelred was a well-trained Thomist theologian who could usually be counted on to speak on some subject—how God brings good out of evil, for instance-- sufficiently abstruse to lose most of us in the first five minutes. He had written a book called *Zen Catholicism*, and that evening he told us, "Put your hands together, and extend your fingers fully.

Feel the pulse of one hand beat to the pulse of the other. Breathe in and out. Pay attention to your breath. Let your mind go still. Focus on a word or phrase. Let your minds relax and journey into a zone of contemplation."

The first reaction to these instructions from 220 teenagers was a good bit of giggling with frequent farting noises thrown in. But then everyone got into it, and the chapel went quiet. I remember having a detached floating sensation and, despite the increasingly bitter cold outside, felt warmer inside than I had all Fall. It was over very quickly. Then Playboy Playmates and Miss Subway bathing beauties swarmed back into my head, but that was a zone I wanted to find again. "That's the best thing that's happened at this place," Tommy said. We talked about it a lot after lights out and soon were exchanging D.T. Suzuki's books on Buddhism and C.J. Jung's *Man and His Symbols*.

There was a road leading somewhere. The trick might be not so much worrying about finding it as just getting on it, even if you didn't know you had.

The term finally ended, and we decamped to our homes. I saw Antonioni's *Blow-Up* that spring vacation and *Farenheit 451*, which later actually got shown at school, because, the Headmaster, a brilliant but dour physicist named Father Leo who had worked on the atomic bomb at Los Alamos before entering the monastery, thought it had a pro-reading message. (On the other hand he refused to screen *If*, because in the final scene English public schools boys machine-gun their Headmaster, and Father Leo disapproved of that message).

1967 had begun with Canada celebrating the 100th anniversary of the British North America Act, the centerpiece of which was the Expo 67 World's Fair. Louis Leakey had announced the discovery of pre-human fossils in the Kenyan Rift Valley. Green Bay had beaten Kansas City in the first of what would be later named the Super Bowls, and Father Leo had actually let us watch it as "a match" of some interest. The Velvet Underground released their first album, a commercial failure that was later much acclaimed. In April the Six-Day War broke out between Israel and its Arab neighbors. *A Man for All Seasons* won the Oscar for Best Picture on April 10th, and the next week there were large demonstrations against the Vietnam War in San Francisco and New York. Fairport Convention played their first gig in Golders Green in late May, and on June 1st, just before we finished our first academic year, The Beatles released *Sgt. Pepper's Lonely Hearts Club Band*. As the spring term ended, the quavering vibrato of "I'd Love To Turn You *Onnnn*," boomed out of every stereo speaker in the school. Was it coincidental that by this time the Portsmouth merchants refused to stock any more Freon?

1967 was a year when 50,000 demonstrated against the Vietnam War at the Lincoln Memorial, but 500,000 marched down Fifth Avenue to *support* it. A vastly outnumbered Israeli army beat off the surrounding Arab forces. The Shah of Iran crowned himself, but King Constantine was kicked out of Greece. The witty Surrealist painter, Rene Magritte, whom Father Hilary called a minor genius, died. China exploded an atomic bomb.

Christiaan Barnard performed the first heart transplant operation in Cape Town. And Mohammed Ali was indicted for refusing the draft with a naïve eloquence that spoke for many and infuriated more: "I ain't got nuthin' against no Viet Congs."

I had no idea how I fit into any of it.

6.

I spent the early summer taking driver's ed at the local high school on Long Island, working what odd jobs I could find and trying unsuccessfully to charm the girls on Atlantic Beach.

That summer Solicitor General Thurgood Marshall was nominated as the first African –American justice of the United States Supreme Court. In July, The Bee Gees released their first album in the UK, and later that month Detroit exploded into one of the worst race riots in American history.

Later in July the family went to Eaton's Ranch in Wolf, Wyoming.

We rode in the mornings high into the Little Big Horns, swam and played softball in the afternoons and rode again after supper as the golden sunsets glanced against the red sandstone hillsides, sometimes encountering small Indian bands, grave and watchful. Then we would square dance at the Lodge with the dude girls, the cowboys and the waitresses and, once or twice, share innocent kisses in the moonlight. I loved the openness of the landscape and the people, the smell of wood burning in the morning, and, most of all, when invited by the working cowboys, rising in the pre-dawn blackness to wrangle the horses left to graze in the high pastures, galloping through the piney woods at a hard clip, until we emerged into the higher meadows fringed with rose-colored clouds on the far ridges.

In August Pink Floyd released their first album, and Fleetwood Mac made their debut at the Windsor Jazz and Blues Festival. George Lincoln Rockwell, leader of the American Nazi Party, was assassinated. And no sooner were we back at Portsmouth than Jim Morrison and The Doors defied the CBS censors by singing the word "higher" from their #1 hit, *Light My Fire*.

By the second year at Portsmouth, Tommy and I surmised that it was a pretty weird place. What kind of school could simultaneously house Benedictine monks living out a life of poverty and prayer, and a math teacher, Ernest Fandreyer, a former Luftwaffe pilot who made a highly visible point of attacking his mouth after every meal with a 14 carat gold toothpick?

When we summoned the courage to complain about his backbreaking homework assignments, Herr Fandreyer would smile jovially and say, "But *everyone* should assign two hours of homework a night!"

What kind of monastery could contain characters like Father Andrew, who tended the lice-infested hen house lovingly by day, but when blackbirds flew through the chapel's broken windows at the consecration, crossed himself and muttered audibly, "Fucking grackles."

Then there was Brother Basil was a gnomish little man with hair growing thickly from his nose and ears. He had never taken final vows because he believed himself to be unworthy and occasionally disappeared to play in high stakes bridge tournaments and go on a spree in New York. In addition, he was an often-exhausting expert on the intermarriages of Europe's noble families.

One of his endearing eccentricities sprang from a deathly fear of lightning. Let an electrical storm appear anywhere on the weather map from Maine to Cape May, and Brother Basil would not walk outside. At the same time he refused to impose upon anyone at school to help him get around. Instead, he would ring up Newport Taxi and have one of its cabs drive the eight miles to the campus and pick him up at the library, drop him off at the monastery thirty seconds later, and make the twenty minute drive back into Newport.

There were younger monks—novices they were called— as well. One was caught cavorting with one of the dining room waitresses by the Bay and went away. Another spent a great deal of time commenting on how well or poorly various of the monks wore their black habits. He moved on, and a charitable silence was strictly maintained.

And yet there was a core of two dozen diligent, devout, highly intelligent and seemingly sane men who had freely chosen to follow a Rule laid down by St. Benedict in the seventh century. They rose before dawn to pray Matins, reconvened for Lauds, Terce, Prime, Vespers and Compline. In between they taught and coached in the School, worked outdoors, pursued their own scholarly and spiritual studies, and still had time to take an interest in us.

When Father Damian was not engaged in extracting honey from the several thousand bees he kept at the

Farm he taught us English. His essential kindliness did not prevent him from drilling us mercilessly on grammar and vocabulary. To this day, I cannot see the word "ephemeral" without hearing him bark, "Brief! Fleeting! Lasting but a day!"

We read from *Beowulf* and Chaucer all the way to Eliot and Pound, although Fr. Damian lingered lovingly on the sprung rhythm of Gerard Manley Hopkins:

> *The world is charged with the grandeur of God.*
> *It will flame out, like shining from shook foil;*
> *It gathers to a greatness, like the ooze of oil crushed.*
> *Why do men then now not reck his rod?*
> *Generations have trod, have trod, have trod...*

In History of Music, Father Ambrose illustrated from the piano and with rare recordings how Gregorian chant and the melodic, one-voice music of the troubadours gave way to the *ars nova* in which two or more melodies could be combined, leading to the establishment of polyphony and counterpoint, and the flowering, in the 16th century, of Orlando Lasso, Josquin des Pres and Palestrina.

In Christian Doctrine, Father Philip led us through the elements of Christian Faith, starting with outlines of the philosophy of Plato and Aristotle. Porter was particularly keen on the fourth century Gregory of Nyssa's concept of the spiritual life as an ascent to God in which the greater knowledge one gains of the Almighty the greater the realization of His mystery. Tommy delighted in Thoreau's defense of the morality of civil disobedience that resonated relevantly then with the intensification of the war in Vietnam. We studied the process of the proper formation of conscience, the obligation to seek information, advice and arrive at a reasoned judgment before taking a specific action, and the occasional need to invoke the principle of probabilism when we could not otherwise decide on a right course. And while that didn't make any of us less venal, petty or self-centered in the short run, it did make us realize that ultimately life was to be treated seriously.

This sense would occasionally arise, between stifled yawns, at symbolic moments of the Mass as well, such as the Offertory. There was, I remembered from Christian Doctrine classes, a prophetic relation between the offering of bread and wine by the High

Priest Melchisedech in the Old Testament and the Last Supper of Jesus. After Abraham had rescued his nephew Lot from the four hostile kings who had fallen on and robbed him, Melchisedech, King of Salem (Jerusalem), brought forth bread and wine and proclaimed, "Blessed be Abram by the Most High God." He did so not merely as refreshment, for Abram (as he was still known) and his men had captured much booty, but as a food offering. Still later, the prophet Malachias foretold the abolition of all the ancient Levitical sacrifices and the institution of an entirely new, "true and real," sacrifice in the days of the Messiah to come, which, more than two millenia later, was what we were still watching unfold in front of us now.

The vestments worn by the celebrant went back to early Judaism or even earlier, to Pagan times.

There was the cincture, the belt, and the maniple, a band worn on the left arm near the wrist. Finally there was the chasuble, the richly embroidered sleeveless outer garment. What was going on in this church had been happening for almost 2,000 years in other churches around the world, and elements of the ceremony had been happening in temples or at altars for thousands, or even tens of thousands, of years before that.

That there was any continuity left at all struck me as amazing, in a world of instant communications and immediately manufactured mass culture. But the *raison d'etre* of a Portsmouth education, as Father Hilary patiently explained, had always been to learn and preserve the wisdom of the past so as to build the best possible present and future. It wasn't a point we immediately embraced. Instead, we rushed, headlong and heedlessly, into the age in which we found ourselves ever more embroiled…

Bill Crimmins' course in Medieval History was more high-spirited, focusing on battles from Constantine's victory at the Mulvian Bridge in 312 through the Crusades to the fall of Constantinople in 1453. Crimmins also covered the rise of the religious orders and the growth and schisms of the Medieval Church; but with his own innate humanism he would point out that the Council of Trent (1570) had declared: "Whoever does what within him lies, God will not deny the necessities of salvation." His excitement with History's sweep was infectious. And along the way Crimmins gave bonus points for victories in athletics, which our first year was problematic since we had a *defeated* season in junior varsity football. In the last game

Coach Crimmins stood on the sideline saying, "Just one victory will save the whole season." As the long afternoon waned Crimmins shifted to, "Just one score…" Finally he pleaded, "Just one sustained drive.…" It was not to be, but he never gave up hope. Nor did he ever hesitate to interrupt a practice or lecture when he saw a student daydreaming. "MacGuire! Are we thinking about football? Or is it Alice again?" We thought he had an uncanny ability to read minds.

We were no longer the youngest at Portsmouth now and settled back into the School routine with something like familiarity.

The courses Father Hilary taught that year were geared at the upper form students, but he led morning and evening prayers for everyone in Saint

Bede's and gave us all talks on the need to cultivate an inner dialogue with God while living fully in the world around us. He emphasized the hopelessness of our situation unless we acknowledged our inherent sinfulness and urged us to be open to the mystery of God's saving Grace. "Thou hast made us for Thyself,'" he would declaim, "and our heart is restless until it rests in Thee." And as if to underscore the point he scrupulously followed the monastic horarium of prayer despite his many other duties at the Farm and in the School.

At the time, of of course, I wasn't at all sure what Father Hilary did mean, or what Grace really was, but I knew he thought it was important, and that therefore I should try to understand it. He took an interest in each of us personally but had at the same time an innate sense of discretion and recognized the need for boys to work through adolescence on their own. On one occasion that Fall, however, he intervened.

I suppose he had spoken to my mother after my fairly dismal first report card had gone out in October, and that she had mentioned my father's deepening depression. All I know is that one day he came astride me as we were walking to lunch, took me completely naturally and companionably by the arm and said, "I thought we might offer early Mass tomorrow morning for your father, that rather heroic figure."

It was not necessarily the first phrase I would have used to describe Dad, but Father Hilary putting it that way made me think anew. And I did serve his Mass, before dawn had broken, in a side altar of the school church. I had been an altar boy for several years in the little parish we went to on Long Island, but serving Hilary in the pre-dawn of the Rhode Island winter in Pietro Belluschi's understated masterpiece, the other monks saying their private Masses at side altars nearby, was a more ethereal and profound experience. I couldn't help notice the small sculpture of a salamander to the side of our altar, and, after we had finished and were walking to breakfast, I asked Father Hilary about it.

"It was recovered from the ruined Abbey of Cluny and sold by a Parisian dealer to Father Hugh at Portsmouth's founding for the express purpose of linking the new monastery school in America with the most famous monastic foundation of the Middle Ages."

Once again, the message was transmitted: Time was eternal, the present temporary, always informed by the past, as it led to a future, yet unseen.

I don't know if that Mass helped my Dad or not, but I felt privileged that Father Hilary and I had done it together. And when the wave of long concealed priestly sex abuse cases broke across the country in 2002, I thought back to that morning and to the many other acts of selfless charity the monks of Portsmouth bestowed upon us in those years: And I wanted to break the neck of every priest rapist with my bare hands.

1967 hurtled toward its conclusion. In October Desmond Morris published *The Naked Ape*, and *Hair* premiered on Broadway. (Informed it included frontal nudity in the theatre for the first time, Jack Benny asked, "Were any of them Jewish?") Tens of thousands of protesters marched on Washington to protest the Vietnam War, and Alan Ginsberg unsuccessfully chanted to levitate The Pentagon. U.S. Navy pilot John McCain was shot down over North Vietnam. In November The Beatles released *Magical Mystery Tour*, including such songs as "All You Need is Love," "Penny Lane," and "Strawberry Fields Forever." In December, Jimi Hendrix released *Axis: Bold as Love*, and The Rolling Stones *By Their Satanic Majesties Request*.

V. 1968

1.

A new era began that winter of 1968. When we came back from Christmas vacation we were only dimly aware that a former seminarian-turned-senator was challenging a President of his own party over the government's Vietnam policy. A hirsute French teacher named Mr. Cable began wearing a *McCarthy For President* button on campus. At first, he was the butt of gentle jokes.

But when Eugene McCarthy, with little funding and no establishment backing, polled more than 40% of the New Hampshire primary vote that February, the campus was electrified. Throughout New England students galvanized into a "Children's Crusade." Mr. Cable, Father Hilary, Bill Crimmins and his striking but histrionic wife, Anne, gleefully joined the fray, driving us into neighborhoods of Tiverton, Fall River, and New Bedford we had never seen to collect petition signatures from and pass out bumper stickers to people we had never met. The headmaster, Father Leo, tried to dissuade us, concerned that such activism would be disruptive to our studies, and from that time on we nicknamed him "Bad Vibes," or Vibes for short. Whereas days before Tommy, Porter and I had been lamenting our animal state after reading *Lord of the Flies* or perfecting our existential funks whilst laboring through *L'Etranger*, now we found ourselves mad with meaning.

So did someone else. As soon as McCarthy proved there was significant support for an anti-war insurgency, Robert Kennedy threw his hat into the ring as well. Now the junior senator from New

York, Kennedy had infinite finances and even greater ambition. Democrats were divided by the development. E.J. Dionne, a year ahead of us, saw McCarthy as a saint and Kennedy as an opportunist (as if that were unusual for a politician); others perceived RFK as the candidate with the necessary bucks and clout to run successfully against LBJ. We spent hours arguing about it in common room bull sessions.

Then in late March President Johnson, looking old and beaten, wimped out of running for re-election. What had been a civilized campaign disintegrated into a cat fight. Although Kennedy had attended Portsmouth for three years, the campus was solidly behind McCarthy. Father Hilary was the principal exception.

"Senator McCarthy has demonstrated moral courage of the first order, but he is far too inscrutable a personality and a politician to attract national appeal," Hilary said. "Kennedy, on the other hand, represents an identifiable liberal tradition that can reach across ethnic and interest groups to build a winning coalition."

My brother Schuyler married his childhood sweetheart Dean Tyndall that winter. He had returned from the Army in Germany in time for a raucous Thanksgiving engagement party at my parents' house. When he came in the front door from Fort Dix still in his uniform, a cheer rang out through the house, except in the corner where one of my best childhood friends stood. Carolyn Carpenter, whose brother George had died the previous January in Vietnam, burst into involuntary tears. It was heart-wrenching. After a period of commiseration superintended most sincerely by my mother and the other guests, the party went on, and the wedding in February was no less festive, too festive for a sixteen year-old inexperienced with alcohol. I had brought my first "A" in an essay—on *The Merchant of Venice*—home to show off, but before I could I had barfed all over it. My father had to help me into the shower to clean up after the festivities. I had a lot to learn.

When in March President Johnson mandated that all computers purchased by the Federal government support the ASCII character encoding, no one noticed. We were more interested in "Danny the Red" and his French compatriots occupying the administrative offices of the University of Nanterre and setting off a chain reaction of demonstrations that would culminate with one million marching through the streets of Paris, and a counter-march of De Gaulle supporters shortly thereafter. Columbia University students occupied their administrative offices and shut down the Morningside Heigths campus as well.

That was a bad spring. I had screwed up, as was so often to be the case, in my studies, and to make me focus on them as opposed to the presidential campaign Father Hilary sent me down to study hall again. When I returned at ten one night, my roommate that year, Sandy Grant, opened the door for me. He had a strained look on his face.

"Have you heard the news?"

"What?"

"They got Martin Luther King."

"You're shitting me."

"He was shot outside his Memphis hotel." I went into my room in silence, in a world that seemed even more messed up than usual. That night I thought of what King had said in a sermon I had read in the papers just two months before:

> "I don't want a long funeral. Say that Martin Luther King tried to love somebody.... Say that I was a drum major for justice. Say that I was drum major for peace, that I was a drum major for righteousness, and all the other shallow things won't matter. I won't have any money to leave behind. I won't have the fine and luxurious things to leave behind. But I just want to leave a committed life behind."

I promised myself that night I would try to do the same, though I had no idea how. The next night, in a debate on a college campus far to the south, Julian

Bond asserted that Dr. King's death proved that America was not worth saving. Tears streamed down William F. Buckley's face as he argued in opposition, but there were few students anywhere who would have agreed with Buckley then.

My admiration for Bobby Kennedy began to grow when I read what he had to say on King's death at a rally in Indiana.

> Martin Luther King was shot and killed tonight….Aeschylus wrote, "In our sleep, pain which cannot forget falls drop by drop upon the heart until, in our own despair, against our will, comes wisdom through the awful grace of God."
> What we need in the United States is not division or hatred; what we need in the United States is not violence of lawlessness, but love and wisdom, and compassion towards one another, and a feeling of justice

toward those who still suffer in this country, whether they be white or black....

The advance man for one-time segregationist George Wallace's campaign arrived at Portsmouth the next week. Marvin George, an African-American football prodigy from New Orleans, and a bunch of us decided to picket the speech. We made signs, marched around the auditorium and then out into the open air, leaving only the Headmaster, two or three other faculty and a handful of students in the place. Later Father Leo accused us of violating the Wallace supporters' freedom of speech.

"What about our freedom of speech?" Marvin asked.

"You don't have any."

"You mean this isn't a democracy?"

"That's exactly what I mean. This is a school, and those of us running it are *in loco parentis* to you boys. That means we make the rules, and yours is not to reason why. And furthermore, we offer hospitality to our guests, even when we disagree with them."

"We were courteous," Porter interjected. "We left him alone."

I tried to focus on my studies for exams, but after the long winter the weather was finally good, and I loved spending every moment I could out of doors. I played varsity tennis that year, and I can still smell the fresh salt air whipping off the Bay as the wind played havoc with the balls. You learned to aim your toss about six feet west of where you really wanted the ball to land on those windy days, and then watched the gusts bend it back. The wisteria that grew on the Manor House trellis perfumed the surrounding air. Summer was coming, but never quite arrived. I sat in classes and dreamed I wasn't there. I couldn't wait any longer, but I had to, because summer was far more patient than I.

Tommy's mother came up for a weekend to visit. She was tall, blonde, irreverent, chic and glamorous, even for a friend's mother. Father Hilary had her into dinner one night and turned out one of his signature cheese souffles. Afterwards he invited Tommy and me in for desert, and the two adults treated us to a discourse in liberal thought. "What was wrong with Adlai Stevenson in 1952?" Hilary exclaimed at one point, and his vehemence made me realize he had drunk a lot of wine. After Mrs. Murray left for her hotel he confided to Tommy, "You know, I'm not supposed to say this, but she just does something to me." Tommy immediately passed that *bon mot* along. We giggled at its absurdity. How hilarious!

At the end of that term Tommy and I had demerits to work off from various minor miscreancies if we didn't want to be held over into the summer vacation. We cleaned the oceanic expanse of windows at Saint Bede's with newspapers for three days while the seniors finished their finals and prepared for graduation. The last morning we packed our bags and said our goodbyes. Father Hilary was preoccupied marking exams but gave us warm wishes for a well-spent summer. Our prefect crunched my fingers a final time, and by way of farewell asked, "So what's the big summer project? Hitting puberty? Answer me in two words—yes or no?"

"That's three," I replied and received a final nougie that left a black and blue mark on my shoulder for weeks to come.

2.

We were drinking beer at a 21st birthday party for my brother Kevin and his Georgetown friends outside the little yacht club on Long Island two weeks later. Suddenly a girl burst from her Mustang and cried, "Omigod, I can't believe it. They got Bobby." It was the night of the California Primary, and, as Robert Kennedy had exited his victory speech in the Ambassador Hotel ballroom in Los Angeles, Palestininan Sirhan Sirhan had shot him as he passed through the kitchen. I rushed home. My mother, who had angrily called Kennedy a carpetbagger when he came to New York to run against Kenneth Keating for the Senate, was in tears in front of the television.

It wasn't until the following morning that we learned that Bobby Kennedy had died. In the days that followed we lined up before dawn well east of Park Avenue so as to file past his casket at St.Patrick's Cathedral. Later we staked out a place on Fifth Avenue where the hearse would pass by on its way to Penn Station after the Requiem Mass, surrounded by people of every color singing, "The Battle Hymn of the Republic." Women cried freely; men hid their tears behind sunglasses; even the cops on duty took frequent swipes across their faces with their meaty forearms. City bus drivers pulled over to the curbs and idled so that passengers could pile out and stand on the sidewalk as a sign of respect. Whatever one might have thought about

Bobby Kennedy's opportunism, he had possessed a magic for setting others on fire with the possibility of building a better world, and of uniting them momentarily, albeit by his death.

Tommy and I spoke on the phone and asked each other, "When does it end? When does all this shit end?" And, over my parents' objections, on a steamy Sunday soon afterwards I jumped on an early train to Washington and joined the Poor People's March. The Mall was packed with protestors, many of whom had been camped out in Resurrection City for weeks, and the Reverend Ralph Abernathy appeared in coveralls, pledging to carry on Dr. King's crusade. "We shall overcome," thundered across the nation's TV sets, hundreds of thousands of black and white Americans with arms interlocked singing as loudly that night as they had the day King gave his "I Have a Dream" speech five years before. But there was a sadness to it all that would take decades to erase.

That night I stayed with Tommy at his mother's beautiful pale-yellow townhouse on 35th Street in Georgetown. To my surprise, Father Hilary was there as well, en route to his holiday in Sicily and southern Italy. Dressed in a well-tailored clerical suit rather than his monk's robes, he was describing the exhibition of American painters he had seen at the Corcoran Gallery that day. When Mrs. Murray came down stairs, he got to his feet and, when we malingered, gave a look that stood us up as well. The doorbell rang, and the other guests arrived. Mrs. Murray served us gin and tonics and pistachios in her book-lined living room filled with upholstered furniture that her toy poodle, Adlai, could not contain restrain himself from jumping on. Her guests-- a diplomatic couple recently returned from a cultural affairs posting to Paris and David Levine, the political cartoonist for the *New York Review of Books*-- quizzed us on the Poor People's March and What Young People Really Thought quite earnestly until the conversation drifted into the void left by Bobby's death.

At some point we migrated into the purple-lacquered dining room with delicate painted Chinese screens of feeding cranes. While the grown ups argued I ravenously consumed my lamb shish kabob, which was much easier to do once the Japanese housekeeper showed me how to get the meat off the skewers. Wine flowed freely, the adults debated the War and abortion on demand, which Mrs. Murray supported vociferously. "The

Church's teaching is archaic," she said a bit shrilly. "Then so is the Hippocratic Oath," Father Hilary answered, color coming into his face, "But somebody has to defend the defenseless."

The two of them glared at one another and a strained silence fell, until someone changed the subject to an upcoming exhibition of Faberge eggs. I got so warm I was afraid I might throw up in public again. But after the strawberries with Kirsch were consumed Tommy mercifully gave me the high sign, and we retreated to his room as Mrs. Murray led her now not so steady guests back to the living room for *demitasse* and cordials. Upstairs Tommy put *Spirit* on the stereo, and asked, "What is Hilary doing here anyway?"

"How should I know?" I answered and promptly passed out.

3.

Summer passed quickly. I painted houses in June and July. Then, in August, Dad took us all to his grandfather's house in Saratoga for long, cool days of watching hot blooded thoroughbreds work out in the morning before golf and tennis, going racing all afternoon, sitting on the porch afterwards as the crowd walked back from the ancient track down Union Avenue into town, and playing pool in the billiards room on the third floor later in the evening. Elsewhere that summer Intel was founded, the first Special Olympics were held, and Pope Paul published *Humanae vitae*. The Prague Spring was crushed as 750,000 Warsaw Pact troops and 6,500 tanks invaded Czechoslovakia. Richard Nixon and Hubert Humphrey were nominated for president during riot-filled conventions in Miami and

Chicago, during the TV coverage of which on ABC William F. Buckley Jr., our classmate Christopher's father, almost came to blows with his debating antagonist, Gore Vidal. It was a long, hot summer.

September in Rhode Island always had a sweet smell to it, of grass still growing, and the peach and pear and plum and apple orchards bringing forth their abundant fruit. The breeze was warm and carried with it the scent of salt from the Bay. Soon it would grow cooler and then cold and then frigid, but those first weeks of the school year the natural world was mild and beautiful.

On the first day I got back Father Hilary invited me in for a chat during which he explained the background of his long friendship with Mr. Crimmins. "His father drowned in a sailing accident when Bill was just three, poor boy. Then Crimmins suffered the terrible tragedy of losing not one but both older brothers in the War. He acted out and eventually we had to fire him from the School, but he went on to get a B.A. from Notre Dame. Afterwards he married a beautiful, and, to all appearances, uncomplicated girl from the Midwest. He was spending all his time in Maine and Palm Beach. Finally, I met him one night in New York and said, 'You can't go on like this. You're wasting your life.' And he said, 'Why not? The one thing I really want to do I can't.' And I said, 'What's that?'

"'Teach at the School.'

"So I told him I'd see what I could do, and that's how he came here. It was the best thing that ever happened to him and to us."

From that moment on Father Hilary treated me as co-conspirator. He still got angry with me when I screwed up, of course, but I always felt that he was on my side. Father Hilary had a sensitivity to psychic pain. In retrospect I suspect it was a subject he knew all too well.

Porter Carroll had gone home to Miami and worked as a grease monkey in a local garage. In his spare time he water skied and fished in Biscayne Bay, played basketball and chased "tranquilo" women. Early football went on its immensely sore way, and we lamented on our terminal stiffness and the inscrutability of our aged coach, "The Rookie," who still insisted on running the Single Wing. "Oh man," Porter would groan and silently shake his head.

A week later school began, and Tommy returned. Tommy had meditated in Washington and hung out with his hippie friends at night, playing the drums in a local band. Then his father had brought him over to Europe, and he had received a tutorial in the lush life.

I actually remember parts of that year quite fondly. There was the time, for example, that Porter's family came up from Florida to visit in October and took us out to a huge feast at Christies, then the finest, and virtually only, restaurant in Newport. Mr. Carroll was a polymath lawyer who imparted his breadth of learning with a light touch. Mrs. Carroll grew orchids and tended to the family. And Anne, Porter's skinny younger sister with short brown hair, had come down for the weekend from her first year at Concord Academy in Massachusetts. She was cute, friendly, and bright.

After we had stuffed ourselves with steak and lobster, deep dish strawberry shortcake and large parfaits, Mr. Carroll was driving us back to school, and Porter suggested he turn on the radio. "Let's not," Porter's mother said sweetly, "We're having such a good time talking." We had been talking about Frank Loyd Wright, The National Gallery and James Joyce. Porter reached forward from the back seat and turned on the radio. Immediately a voice boomed out, "HELP STOP VD!" His mother inhaled sharply, and her face reddened. His father turned off the radio. The rest of us almost suffocated suppressing our giggles.

In October African-American athletes Tommy Smith and John Carlos raised their arms in a black power salute after winning the gold and bronze medals in the Olympic 200 metres in Mexico City. Former first lady Jacqueling Onassis married shipping tycoon Aristotle Onassis. And, in November, Yale announced it would admit women.

Another Saturday night later that autumn Porter and I got home from a losing football game to find Tommy waiting for us with a plan for the night's entertainment. Tommy had brought several hits of LSD back from Washington at the beginning of the school year and stowed it wrapped in aluminum foil in a small hole he had dug in the courtyard of St. Bede's. Now he had retrieved it, and in the privacy of his room unwrapped the magic elixir with great pomp and circumstance. Some discolored liquid dribbled out, and there was a microscopic residue of powder on the insides of the foil. Porter smirked, and Tommy conceded, "Apparently my storage technology failed."

"It could have been bad shit," I offered, hoping to make him feel better. Then we all licked the foil to make sure. It tasted like decomposing sneakers. Afterwards we went to the weekly school movie.

"I think I feel something," we whispered back and forth to each other during a soporific showing of *The Red Shoes*. Two hours later, as we took an illegal walk down to the Bay on the brisk fall night, I confessed, "You know, aside from an occasional hard-on during the dance scenes, I didn't feel a fucking thing."

"Maybe it's a late breaking batch," Tommy suggested hopefully.

"Like when?" asked Porter, "The year 2000?"

It so happened that there was a clumsy but kind-hearted day student who played tackle on our team named Rathbone. He was rumored to be a head and after a practice the following week Porter asked him if he could score some acid for us.

"What did you have in mind?" he asked.

"Six hits of sunshine," Porter answered, trying to sound authoritative. It was the only brand name of LSD any of us actually knew. Rathbone thought about it slowly. "I heard, like, there was some of that over in Fall River, but it wasn't cheap."

"How much?"

"Five bucks a hit…"

"Make it three hits in that case."

We got together the small fortune necessary to buy the three tablets and designated the first Saturday afternoon after football ended in November for the lift off. We dropped the acid before lunch and felt the first tremors going through our bodies as Vibes stood up and began to read an exquisitely boring series of announcements. Father Hilary, who had been romancing a wealthy alumnus with sherry in his rooms before lunch for his latest project—a Chinese garden—was slightly redder-faced than usual and groaned, "Oh shut up," as Father Leo segued into the need for water conservation when flushing urinals. What sounded like a solid wall of laughter went running up like a sheet of steel to the dining room roof and hurtled back down again. If only I could have focused my eyes I'm sure I could have seen it.

Afterwards we listened to Moby Grape in the common room and then started walking down past the football fields towards the pond. There was an old dam that was broken through in the middle, but it was wide enough to stand on and throw pebbles into the water. Watching the concentric circles start small and widen gradually until they wandered into the far shore, brought an hypnotic slowness to the world, even as my mind was making/missing a trillion connections in colossal overdrive.

"How you doin'?" Porter asked Tommy.

"OK, I think," he answered slowly, "But the visuals are getting a little intense."

Then the colors really started coming on. Looking at a tree or a rock or a stone wall would reveal a whole range of blues, pinks, purples, reds, corals, fleshes, fuschias, iodines, yellows, reds, roses, greens, cypresses, brasses, cocoas, reds, bays, indigos, bourbons, wheats, irons, reds, browns, blacks, and more reds moving from a central color, oscillating and pulsing. I was suddenly dizzy and uncertain of my footing. I tried to walk off the bridge but so many things were bursting inside my brain I couldn't trust my eyes to see or my feet to follow, so I got down on my hands and knees, hugged the edges of the concrete dam and crawled slowly towards the bank as Tommy and Porter laughed uproariously. Once safely back on shore I wallowed in the last cranberry and yellow leaves of fall.

We tramped the woods all afternoon. Hot waves of words holed up in our heads, and colors split in front of our eyes. Whole kingdoms came into being inside our brains and then collapsed. A joint Porter produced "to take the edge off" made us ravenous instead. We went to the Tuck Shop and stuffed ourselves with ice cream as Miles Davis' "Bitches Brew" played on the sound system. At dinner the colors danced off the "rainbow meat" on our plates and jumped onto the redwood beams that arched above us. The movie that evening was *West Side Story*, and the dancers looked slightly ridiculous as they leapt through the city streets, changing colors. When I tried to sleep that night my mind still raced wild. There was a raw and ragged feeling in my gut as well.

In the morning I dressed and struggled up to the chapel. As the last of the drug was working through my system, the Mass began. The chanting sounded otherworldly weird. I remember the consecration in particular. The crowd of priests gathered around the altar, the music stilled, the congregation silent and intent. And yet all I could summon up that morning was a big, "So what?"

> *This is my body.*
> So what.
> *This is my blood.*
> So?
> *Do this in memory of me.*
> Why?

It was the first time I had ever felt that way. I may not always have been enthusiastic about church before then, but it was part of the schedule. Now I felt totally estranged. It was the acid speaking, I suppose.

...I'm not sleepy and there ain't no place I'm going to,
Hey, Mr. Tambourine Man, play a song for me
In the jingle jangle morning I'll come following you

Take me on a trip upon your magic swirling ship...

But it wasn't the last time I had that experience, and LSD had less to do with it as time went on.

3.

School work intensified in what was the all important junior year for college admission. I had never read or written so much. Shakespeare, Swift, Dryden, Pope, and Fielding finally gave way to the Romantics, the Brontes, Dickens, Hardy and into the 20th century. However even-tempered he may have been personally, Father Damian was a taskmaster when it came to work. He made us write a composition every day, and a ninety-minute double period essay in class once a week. It came back within forty-eight hours, meticulously corrected, analyzed and critiqued, and thanks to his determination even the most "indolent, insolent and ignorant" among us learned to write.   But it was the poetry I really enjoyed:

> *Oh stay at home my lad,*
>   *And plow the land and not the sea,*
> *And leave the soldiers to their drill*
> *And all about the idle hill*
> *Come shepherd sheep with me.*

And I also loved studying American history with Bill Crimmins. That year we went at a dizzying pace from the Colonial Era to the Kennedy Admnistration. When we weren't studying our textbook and memorizing dates, Crimmons made us read Frederick Jackson Turner on the closing of the American frontier, Richard Hofstadter on the Paranoid Style in American Politics, and George Santayana on the Lessons of History. One November afternoon Crimmins gave a blow by blow account of the Battle of Rhode Island, which took place along Bloody Run, the brook on

Narragansett property that fed into the pond. He pointed out the stone markers of Hessian graves, and acted out the officers on both sides of the battle.

In the Upper Form common room we argued about whether the Civil War was fought over slavery or states' rights, whether Melville or Twain best captured the 19th century American spirit, whether idealism or imperialism impelled us overseas in the Spanish-American War right up to Vietnam, and whether Capitalism could ever be compatible with a just society.

"In the Gospel of Mark," Tommy asserted passionately, "Jesus said, "If you have a second coat in your closet, you must give it to your brother.'"

"You don't even believe in him," Porter shot back, running his hand through his blonde hair. "And besides, it was Luke."

But Tommy would not back down. He quoted from a red-bound book called *Quotations from Chairman Jesus*:

> If a brother needs clothes or food to get through the day, and one of you says, "Go in Peace. Be warm, be full," without giving them what they need, what good is it? Faith by itself, without doing something about it, is a dead thing." (James 2:15-17)

"Yeah," Porter answered, "Too bad not everyone can afford to be a Commie."

Tommy lunged at him then with surprising strength for a non-athlete and wrestled Porter to the ground. They struggled for awhile until Father Hilary emerged from his room, peered over his half glasses, and asked, "What is going on?"

That ended the contest of conflicting ideas for the day.

What had started out as a pretty good year, however, was complicated by the fact that Father Hilary, had imported his prefects for the year from another house to shore up lax discipline in the Sixth Form. He had been especially irate when he heard rumors of mutual masturbation sessions in that class. Under Hilary, Saint Bede's was supposed to be a refuge of sophistication, and though this was belied a thousand times each day by some form of barbarism, there was a kernel of truth to it. Other houses had electronic geeks, pool sharks and surreptitious soap opera fans. In Saint Bede's even a crypto hot rod enthusiast like Porter was supposed to read Muriel Spark, see Bunuel movies and be able to talk knowledgeably about James Brown.

Whereas the prefects that descended upon us favored *Love Story* and The Monkees. The Monkees! There was friction from the start and an uneasy truce at the best of times. And Richard Nixon's election, with the smallest margin of victory since 1912, only heightened the sense of frustration felt on campus. At lunch one day, Tommy said his mother was considering moving abroad, and Father Hilary chimed in that only his vow of stability stood in the way of him joining her.

I had certainly felt depressed before, but it was nothing like I went through that junior year. The walls closed in on me, a bevy of black clouds descended into my brain, and I felt as if I was miles apart from everything, including myself. Words reached me through a fog. It was as if I were watching my own life from far off, and I wasn't doing anything well. The thought recurred that I was on an inexorable path to end up like my poor father. Was it growing up—adolescence—or some congenital condition I was helpless to do anything about? I didn't know, but it scared me, and I felt frightened when I felt as if I could feel anything at all. Father Hilary noticed something amiss early on and began inventing excuses for me to come into his room for a toasted corn muffin and a glass of juice. Since I could not articulate what was going on inside we could hardly discuss it, but I knew he knew. And I will also be grateful for how reassuringly he handled those sessions.

About that time, I became friendly with an auburn-haired underformer in Saint Bede's. Consagra was a jock, muscle-bound and athletic in his movements, with a ready smile and a cocky swagger. Occasionally he visited my room for help with his homework. As time went on, I would visit him in his, and we'd have mock wrestling matches. Was it homoerotic? Did Rose Kennedy wear a black dress?

Not long after Father Hilary called me in one day. Very indirectly, after discussing several other topics, he came quietly to the point, "I've heard there may be some homosexual attraction abroad in the School. I feel keenly for those going through such a phase. We had to dismiss a boy several years ago when he could not stop acting out and interfering with others. It was a shame, because he would have been one of our first Black graduates. The teaching of the Church is not that homosexuality is intrinsically wrong, you know. Some people are just born that way. It's not any fault of theirs. But because it is not part of the natural order, the Church teaches that those who are primarily homosexual must not act on their disordered urges." He paused for a moment and continued quietly, "I knew Maurice Bowra and admired him. It's difficult to deal with, especially for young people; but contemplating the spirituality of obedience is always a good place to start."

I didn't know who Bowra was then and wasn't sure what any kind of spirituality had to do with the polymorphous fantasies I had gleefully allowed to sprout up in our separation from the world of women. And it wasn't a topic I was likely to broach with friends. I didn't, in fact, really know what I thought of homosexuality—was it wrong, as we'd always been taught, or was it like being left-handed? Or maybe being gay was both, which didn't sound fair, not that in my present mood I thought anything was. But, in any event, I was pretty sure it wouldn't solve my problems. Yet the fact that Father Hilary thought the subject was worth discussing seriously with a sixteen year-old made an impression on me.

On the other hand, heterosexual contact was infrequent and usually dissatisfying, too. We would have dances with girls' schools that at their best passed for perfumed football scrimmages, Vibes running around with his ruler to assure that we maintained a six inch distance from our partners as we tried to wrap ourselves around each other. We wrote letters to girls we had met, and occasionally they answered them. I got one from a sweet, blonde-haired Ethel Walker's student I had met at a holiday dance. Carla was her name. There was a wax seal on the back of the envelope that read "SWAK."

"What does that mean?" I asked Tommy.

"*Sealed with a kiss*, you lucky moron. Does your mother put that on every letter she writes?"

During the Christmas vacation that year, the Rolling Stones released *Beggars Banquet*, and I succeeded in getting Carla to come in from Greenwich for a hamburger and to a movie with me in New York. Unfortunately it was *Midnight Cowboy*, highly recommended by Porter, and when it got to the scene where John Voight is sucked off for five bucks in a Times Square porn cinema, beautiful Carla sweetly, but in a voice near breaking, asked, "Can we leave now? I just remembered I have to be home early."

And so it went....

VI. 1969

1.

One of the highlights of house life in Saint Bede's was the party Father Hilary threw each St. Hilary's Day, lighting up the depths of the January 13th winter's night in honor of his namesake in religion, Bishop of Poitiers, Doctor of the Church, and, until his death in 368, defender of the Divinity of Christ against the heresy of Arianism embraced by the emperors, which denied the divinity of Christ, maintaining he had been created by the Father and was thus neither coeternal or consubstantial with Him. Father Leo was invited, and Hilary made a point of spiking the punch with a little jug wine in his presence, then tasted it and pronounced, "Completely innocuous." In order to celebrate Joe Willie Namath's and the Jets' upset victory over the Baltimore Colts in the Super Bowl the day before appropriately, we went back for as many cups as we could in between multiple portions of cake and ice cream. The occasion became quite jolly. Tommy got up the nerve to ask an unusually cheery Vibes if he could come discuss an idea he had, and Father Leo uncharacteristically answered, "Splendid. Tomorrow. Two PM!"

The next day Tommy presented Father Leo with an idea for a community service program in Newport. What King Solomon called the "heart-gladdening" effect of wine having disappeared by the following afternoon, Vibes immediately erected numerous bureaucratic hurdles and mumbled, "Maybe next year." So Tommy went back to the work squad, clearing brush from the woods and keeping the grounds clean, affording everyone on it a little fresh air and ample opportunity to smoke cigarettes.

But when Father Hilary heard that Tommy wanted to start a volunteer service program and that Vibes had vetoed it, he sprung into action. Hilary and his sheep dog, Lad, found Tommy by the pond clearing some branches from the Hessian graves, collared him and said, "I want to see you in my room right now."

When they got there Hilary sat him at his desk and said, "I understand you want to do some useful work in Newport."

"I wanted to, but when I asked Father Leo…"

"I have spoken to Father Leo. I don't understand why you didn't come to me first, but in any case, when you have a good idea—an important idea—you cannot give up so easily. I've jotted down a list of numbers on the pad there. Now start calling them, and let's see what happens."

Half an hour later Tommy had spoken to two day care centers, an old people's home and the juvenile delinquency mentoring office. They had all requested volunteers. The program Tommy had dreamed of had been launched. When he put down the phone and looked over to Father Hilary, he was grinning.

"Father, how did you do that?"

"I hardly did anything at all. It was your idea, that was the most important part, and now you've just made it happen. I just called one or two friends who knew where you should start. Let that be a lesson to you. Never let anyone tell you a good idea can't become reality. It can. And in this case it would be immoral if it didn't."

When Tommy and the other guys began tutoring grade schoolers, playing ball with teenage offenders and reading to old folks the following week, it was Father Hilary and Bill Crimmins who drove them in and out of Newport. Later, as the program grew, many more of us got involved in some way or another, whether we were playing sports or not. We enjoyed our work and those we came to know. It made us feel there was a way to make things better at a time conventional politics presented a dead end, and even the counter-culture (Jim Morrison was arrested for indecent exposure at a Doors concert in Florida that March) was veering out of control. And, unexpectedly, it helped me wrestle low spirits to a standstill, by looking outside of my own immense self-absorption, and made it possible to turn toward the looming light of Spring.

One other great thing happened in the School that Spring. Portsmouth instituted a program of independent study. After the mountains of memorization and skill-acquisition we had endured we were finally given a chance to pursue something of our own design. Tommy became an apprentice at Trinity Rep, the excellent theater in Providence. He did every kind of grunt work they gave him in the front of the house and backstage. He took acting and voice lessons and wrote a series of dramatic scenes. He came back from the first production he worked on—an O'Casey play-- and sang the title air nightly in the corridors of Saint Bede's:

> *A sober black shawl hides her body entirely,*
> *Touched by the wind and salt spray of the sea.*

> *Down in the darkness a slim hand so lovely,*
> *Carries a rich bunch of red roses for me.*

And the cat calls these renditions occasioned were deafening but undeniably affectionate. When that Spring he was given a bit part in a production of *Midsummer Night's Dream*, set as if it were in a circus complete with high wire acts, Father Damian drove the entire English class up in a bus to see him, and the performance came to a halt for thirty seconds as we applauded his entry. The rest of the audience was bewildered, but the professional acting company joined enthusiastically in the ovation, and from that moment Tommy began to dream of life upon some sort of wicked stage.

Porter in the meantime disappeared into the depths of Father Leo's beloved Science Building. He had worked there often with the other ham radio enthusiasts and then as a disc jockey, hyping up the volume at WJHU, the school's mercifully weak radio station. But now he retreated into a locked room for months, assembling and tinkering with elements from a kit he had ordered and then supplemented with various other components. Whenever I went to visit him there the place looked like a junkyard. But he would wipe his hair out of his face, say everything was tranquilo, and carry on. He was someone who always needed nearly complete chaos before he could feel organized. When he emerged at last that May he had built a rudimentary computer, which he demonstrated to the astonishment of Father Hilary and the only slightly grudging admiration of Vibes.

Others also pursued interesting independent projects-- in urban archaeology, oceanography and writing. Marvin George researched slavery in colonial Rhode Island. I played piano with Father Ambrose, for which I had little talent, yet from which I derived much joy. My other studies left a lot to be desired. I did reasonably well in history and English. I passed biology, too, but mathematics was my undoing. Trig and quadratics left me far behind. A couple of nights before the exam I waited until long after lights out to sneak down to the math department's office in the Manor House. I turned on a single desk lamp and was getting ready to root around in the files to see if I could find an advance copy of the test when out of the stillness a slight shadow crossed the floor. I froze and thought, "This is it."

Then Fr. Andrew's voice— calm, yet stern and ever so slightly mournful-- came out of the darkness: "Is this *really* necessary?"

I couldn't bring myself to look back.

"No, Father."

"Then get back to bed, and I never want to hear this spoken of again."

I did as I was told. Two mornings later I took one look at the final exam and knew it would be hopeless. I wrote down everything I knew or could make a guess at and was lucky to get a 33. That would have to be made up during the summer.

Meanwhile the vacation stretched ahead.

2.

That summer of 1969, I went out to California to work in Sun Valley repairing ski lifts and building cross country skiing trails. I never quite got there. Instead, I settled into the comfort of Tommy's cousin Joe Tobin's Hillsborough home, warmly welcomed by his family. We frequently sprinted down to San Franciso, explored the Haight and took in concerts at the Fillmore, listening to Santana, Spirit, and the likes of Joan Baez singing her salute to Ronald Reagan:

> *He's a drug store truck-driving man,*
> *You know he's the head of his own Ku Klux Klan....*

More than once we arrived home after dawn after hearing the Grateful Dead sing the last of several encores:

> *Lay down dear brother,*
> *Lay down and take your rest,*
> *Won't you lay-ay down,*
> *Upon your Savior's breast....*

The Summer of Love had been declared dead, but alternative papers and radio, new music, hip clothing stores (later that summer Don and Doris Fisher would open the first Gap store on Ocean Avenue) and idiosyncratic people were everywhere. If it was utopian to think there might really be a Revolution, ample evidence abounded that there were already nearly infinite mini-revolutions. One night, Joe took me to a near-by neighbor's for dinner. The Randolph Hearsts had four beautiful daughters at the table that night. One of them was a sweet blonde fifteen year-old named Patty, today the wonderfully resilient Patricia Hearst Shaw, whose defense fund Joe would found after her kidnapping and repeated rape several years later.

Today a lot of people say that in the Sixties people did what they did because they were idealistic. I want to believe that but would also say that we did much of what we did because we were self-indulgent and not always very honest, especially with ourselves. Sure, you can say we did drugs to attain a higher consciousness, and we broke laws to achieve social justice, and we called our parents' generation "pigs," because we were creating "more viable commitments," but from this vantage point it looks like we were doing whatever we felt like.

It didn't seem that way then. I went down to L.A. and spent the night Neil Armstrong walked on the moon watching as Walter Cronkite narrated the event for CBS as it was projected on a sixty foot screen at Disneyland, while riding the "Moon Walk" high in the air, and admiring the full moon in the California sky as it pulsated particularly powerfully, thanks to two hits of Lemon Sunshine. Chappaquidick happened that same week. In contrast to JFK swimming around PT 109 until he had located and saved all of his crew, Teddy couldn't wait to get away from his sunken underwater car with Mary Joe Kopechne trapped in the back seat.

Then I went to my classmate Michael Garvey's house in Springfield, Illinois. His bemused Dad, Hugh Garvey, was the publisher of Templegate Press. He drew on his pipe and quoted Judge Learned Hand as he reflected on the Chappaquidick news: "They saith not a Pater Noster there."

Shortly thereafter, on August 9th, eight months pregnant actress Sharon Tate, coffee heiress Abigail Folger, and others were murdered by followers of Charles Manson on August 9th. The next night they killed again.

Michael and I joined a group sitting in at the Governor's office for social justice in downstate Cairo. We were none too gently carried away. Then, I headed back east to attend a musical camping weekend rumored to be happening on an upstate New York farm. The tickets cost $15 at the local record store in Cedarhurst.

We drove up to Woodstock in Mark O'Neil's magic VW bus. He had rigged up its own loudspeaker and siren system, with which Mark expertly bluffed his way through crowds and check points, claiming we were an emergency vehicle.

"Cool as the breeze," Chris Coy called out emphatically as we made our way in.

By the time we had established our campsite on Friday afternoon Woodstock was a sea of people, the second biggest city, in all of New York State. We wandered over to hear Richie Havens start off the festival, singing the lines of "Freedom" interwoven with "Sometimes I Feel Like a Motherless Child." We found seating near the top of a natural, grassy amphitheatre, crammed with sweating bodies. Most were sporting long hair, bell bottoms and t-shirts, but near us was a group of young Italian-Americans from Arthur Avenue in the Bronx wearing chinos and white short-sleeved shirts with slicked back hair, eating lustily from a mountainous hamper of fried chicken, pastry and soft drinks. The rest of us had ladled ourselves a cup of the tasteless, runny, macrobiotic coucous that was being served for free by scrawny hippie girls down the way. Porter Carroll halfheartedly claimed it was delicious, but after the second soggy slurp, I couldn't help envying our Bronx friends.

We sat peering down the hillside trying to see (our neighbors had also brought binoculars, which looked uncool but was certainly sensible; so many things that looked uncool have turned out to be sensible). Country Joe and the Fish got the crowd dancing on its feet when they played "Rock 'n Soul Music", shouting, "Sock it to me, sock it to me, sock it to me…" Then Arlo Guthrie strummed his acoustical guitar and sang, "Coming into Los

Angeles." He was followed by Shana Na singing, "At the Hop," and then by Country Joe McDonald shouting into the microphone, "Give me an 'F,' give me a 'U,' give me a 'C,' give me a 'K, and what have you got? Nearly a million people in the audience told him what, and then he asked four more times and was answered by thunderous screams of "FUCK." Then he started in:

> *Well it's one, two, three,*
> *What are we fighting for?*
> *Don't ask me I don't give a damn*
> *Next stop is Vietnam....*

The whole festival rose up and united in the choruses then and brought Woodstock to one of its early peaks. That night we walked deep in the woods, hearing the music rise and fall in the distance, bouncing off the trees and the stars.

The next day I listened to John Sebastian sing "I Had a Dream," to an enthusiastic crowd from a smaller stage in the woods. The rains came. The "Mexican" weed we were smoking ("250 miles southwest of Mexico City," Chris Coy had opined after taking his first hit with a *sommellier's* pretension if not his precision—his dealer later admitted to us that the shit was homegrown in New Jersey) kept us wrecked. Porter's black leather uniform was by now severely soaked, and he shivered slightly when he said, "Tra-tranquilo." He also stunned us by saying he had decided not to come back to Portsmouth for his senior year. Vibes and he had decided that four years of boarding school was enough.

It rained harder and harder. Crosby, Stills and Nash sang "Wooden Ships," The Who screamed, "We're Not Gonna Take it," and Joe Cocker belted out, "With a Little Help from My Friends."

Then the deluge began in earnest, and people tried to take cover, tried to move past each other, slipped and slid and finally rose up in a great chorus to propitiate the rain gods with a chant that reached to the heavens. It didn't work. It poured and flooded, and after that the mud flowed into the makeshift tents and soaked us all. Late that night I took refuge in one, crawling on my belly and ignoring the cries of protest. Sleep would have been in short supply, even if I hadn't soon realized that the couple in the sleeping bag next to me were getting it on all night long. In the morning they both turned out to be girls.

The next day it rained some more, but no one cared. Ten Years After sang, "I'm Going Home," and the Jefferson Airplane played "Volunteers." Max Yasgur, the farmer whose land Woodstock was held on, stepped up to the microphone and said, "I'm a farmer, and I don't know how to speak to twenty people, let alone half a million, but I just want to say that for a crowd of kids this size to come here, listen to music and have fun, and only fun, is wonderful, and God Bless you."

Sly and the Family Stone played, "I Want to Take You Higher," Paul Butterfield played "Love March," and we stayed up through the night listening until Jimi Hendrix rang in the druggy dawn and the end of Woodstock with his electric, stoned-out "Purple Haze," followed by his jagged guitar solo of the "Star Spangled Banner."

During the course of the night I got separated from the others, and our camp had been broken up by the mud streams rolling through it, so I hitchhiked home, and in the process partnered up with a stringy blonde-haired, Indian head-banded girl named Vickie who was searching for one of her sandals in the mud. We looked like refugees streaming out of a Balkan war zone. The first seven miles took us eight hours, but then the car we were riding in started to move.

When we got to New York I bought her dinner in a vegetarian restaurant in the East Village and took her to my aunt and uncle's apartment on the upper east side, who were supposed to be out of town for the summer at their rented beach house on Long Island. I demonstrated my savoir-faire by trying to enter her before she had gotten her pants fully off, and she wasted no time in letting me know my technique was seriously wanting. It was my first night.

In the morning my uncle showed up to collect the week's mail. He wasn't happy to see us.
"Good morning."
"Good morning, Uncle Buddy."
"How soon can you be out of here?"
"Right away."

We grabbed our knapsacks and split. At Penn Station we turned to each other to say goodbye, before jumping on different train lines, she to Long Beach and me to Far Rockaway. Despite my maladroitness Vickie was kind. Her last words to me were, "Be good."

I wonder where she is now.

3.

Listen, my son, to your master's precepts, and incline the ear of your heart. Receive willingly and carry out effectively your loving father's advice, that by the labor of your obedience you may return to him from whom you had departed by the sloth of disobedience... (Rule of Saint Benedict, Prologue)

A couple of afternoons later the bus dropped me off at the top of Cory's Lane, and I walked down to the Portsmouth gate. I had been summoned back to make up my disastrous math exam. For the next two weeks I lived life on the monastic model, a curious contrast to Woodstock, both counter-cultural life styles, one energized by the search for a new Way, and the other stabilized by fourteen centuries of experience based upon a seventh century's saint's strict yet loving rule.

In the medieval formulation the monastery was a kind of midpoint between the earth and Heaven, and while that concept might be considered quaint in the latter half of the twentieth century, it was still possible to envision a monastery as a kind of spiritual powerhouse in the world. Like any human endeavor, of course, it had its flaws, but its virtues were manifest, too, as was the very audacity of its mission. "Monasticism is a protest," the Abbot had preached to us the previous Spring. "Not a protest against anything, but a protest *for* God and the things of God."

Father Hilary was on his annual holiday in Italy, taking the waters at Montecatini. It was left to Father Andrew to take on my nearly hopeless cause. He had developed a bump on his forehead and a nervous twitch that jerked his chin sideways every thirty seconds, but his remained one of the most elegant mathematical minds that I have ever known. His ideas came out in torrents and then would hit a snag, but he recovered, carried on and got me to understand what had previously been unfathomable. Frequently he interrupted his lessons to recite one of his endless series of off-color limericks:

> *There once was a lass from Abyerestwyth*
> *Who took grain to the Miller to make grist with,*
> *The Miller's boy Jack put her flat on her back*
> *And they mingled the things that they piss with.*

Within two weeks of this regime he had raised my final examination from 31 to 99. The school refused tuition for the crash course, and Father Andrew appeared embarrassed when afterwards my Mom insisted on sending him a Steuben ashtray as a gift.

What I really remember about those two weeks was rising early in the height of summer to attend Mass (excepting those days when I over-slept and Andrew had to come wake me). We would study math all morning. Then I would swim in the Bay with Father Damian and eat lunch in the monastery in silence as a spiritual text was read by one of the monks. After a twenty-minute period of recreation in which the conversation could range from the day's news to astronomy, archaeology, cartography, eschatology, and the relationship of alchemy to medieval theology, there was a period of prayer. Then I would have a shorter math tutorial in the afternoon and be free to play tennis with Father Bede.

Vespers were at 5:30. In the evenings after dinner we would sit and chat in the calefactory, giving me the chance to hear each of the monk's own unique life's story. Father Wilfred had lived in Greenwich Village near e.e. cummings and danced with Pavlova. He was now a *Rouge Dragon* and the country's foremost heraldic artist. Father Thomas had been ordained in both the Methodist and Episcopal churches before making his way to Rome. Dr. Lally, a retired layman in residence, had taught my father in the 1930s and written an impenetrable study of Lord Acton's opposition to the nineteenth century doctrine of papal infallibility. Father Ambrose was the radiantly kind, genuinely modest and supremely brilliant concert pianist who had given up fame and an international musical career to experience God and teach English and music to nitwits like me.

I sat with them at meals. On those mornings I woke up early enough I assisted at their Mass, and I sometimes stayed to listen to their night prayers echo up into the distant rafters. I wanted to know what drew them to that life. In a way I wanted to be drawn to it to. But I never was drawn. It seemed to me then that spiritual sensations are most often impossible to articulate or to communicate to others—silently experienced impressions that waft away on the air.

How wrong I was, but that took many more years to learn.

Father Andrew was the most brilliant and bizarre of them all. He could rage with language worthy of a sailor he had been in war time one moment and drop to his knees in front of you asking for forgiveness with abject humility the next. One day at the end of class we as usual ended up discussing things far afield, and I asked him how he had come to Portsmouth.

"Before the war I'd been a teacher and started a school in Cambridge. Systems analysis and statistics were both passions of mine, but the problem was I couldn't see much meaning in them anymore. There was a storm rising in me, and this was the one choice I could make to quell it, some of the time. I am a monk and a mathematician and by definition I have one foot firmly in faith and the other in reason. When I solve for 'the equation of life' and I insert the variable of God, it works. Conversely, when I remove the variable of God, nothing works."

His honesty was disarming. Were all revolutions inside the mind only temporary? Tommy often spoke about using Zen to defeat the ego. I had come to the conclusion that you were lucky to wrestle it to an occasional draw.

When I left the monastery and took a small Newport Aero plane back to LaGuardia, the only other passengers were Jimmy and Candy Van Alen, condescending from their Bellevue Avenue

"Cottage" on their way to the second U.S. Open, where Rod Laver would complete his second Grand Slam, this time as a professional, as opposed to his amateur triumph in 1962. Van Alen had saved the Newport Casino from developers, founded the International Tennis Hall of Fame there and revolutionized the sport with his inventions of the tiebreaker and the Van Alen (no let) Scoring System, about which Laver and John Newcombe would later somewhat ungratefully remark in their Aussie accents after a few beers, "You can take VASS and stick it up your arse."

James Van Alen smiled benevolently as we taxied up the runway and complimented my early Jimmy Connors metal racquet, while Candy recited all the upcoming week's parties to him. Theirs was a different world.

I wondered then if, of all the counter-cultural adventures I'd had that summer of 1969, those two weeks of studying with the monks hadn't been the most amazing of all. And the words from St. Benedict's Rule still echoed in my ears:

> *Seek peace and quiet; be much more of a listener than a talker; listen with reverence; if you must speak, speak the truth from your heart. In other words, walk in the presence of God under the guidance of the gospel, in order to see Him who has called us to his kingdom. To start with, ask God for the help of His Grace; then never give up....*

4.

It's easy to circumnavigate years of one's life telling stories that pop out of a brain that probably pre-selected them anyway. Wasn't it George Orwell who wrote that he considered autobiographies to be almost always lies, because they inevitably concentrated on the triumphs of a man's life, whereas, in truth, 95% of anyone's experience consisted of failure and humiliation?

The same could be said for an age. People romanticize the Sixties and wax nostalgic about the drugs, sex, rock and roll, and so-called freedom. But all those things involved as much pain as pleasure. Many of the rock stars died young. Sex was often tortured. The apostles of drug use became their own most compelling rebuttals. We want to believe the Sixties were about unconditional love, giving Peace a chance, Flower Power, and selfless idealism. However, wasn't there also a lot of egotistical attitudinizing, selfishness and unadulterated indulgence? And, if we were really honest, couldn't we say we had felt lonely, uncertain, foolish and miserable much of the time?

I think so.

Father Hilary welcomed us back with his usual end-of-summer high spirits when we arrived for early football our final year at Portsmouth. He told us expansively of his three weeks motoring around Italy and walking the *Cinque Terre*. I in turn told him the expurgated highlights of our time in California and Woodstock.

"I'm not sure Woodstock will be remembered 100 years from now," Hilary commented skeptically, "as anything more than a passing cultural phenomenon."

I mentioned that remark to Bill Crimmins when I saw him and asked if Hilary, normally so broad-minded, wasn't being a bit puritanical. Crimmins looked me in the eye.

"When I was a boy at the school, Hilary was a young monk. During the War he used money from his family trust to start the Farm with 150 hens, sixty Cheviot sheep, pigs, beehives, potatoes and corn. Hilario worked eighteen hours a day, so that when there was no food in the markets of Newport, Fall River, or even Providence, we boys never went hungry. Hilary kept a sheep dog for the flock, and I remember one wonderful Sunday when Rags proudly herded the sheep into the chapel during High Mass. So that Rags wouldn't disturb his monastic brethren Hilary slept in the monastery room closest to the door. It was almost entirely unheated. He slept there for twenty years. The day he moved to become housemaster of Saint Bede's he said, 'This will be the ruin of me.' So however strict you think he can be, I promise you he was always stricter with himself than anyone else."

I was silenced.

Early football with our new coach, former Boston College All American guard Phil Coen, was hard as hell and exhilarating at the same time. We had three two-hour practices a day and then went into chalkboard sessions, film reviews and playbook memorization. Coach Coen installed a new split-T offense with tremendous emphasis on line blocking but plenty of passing as well. As hard work as it was, football became fun and deeply satisfying. The effort paid off, and we started winning games we had never won before and wondering how far we might be able to go.

Tommy arrived back as the school year began, sun-bronzed and filled with stories about his Spanish sojourn. As usual, his arsenal of activities had far outstripped mine. To think, we had been enjoying football!

"And now we're here," I allowed.

"Yeah, I hate this place. Let's leave."

"It's our last year. If we weren't here we'd be stuck in some other prison. Let's try to make the most of it."

Tommy looked at me dubiously.

Father Leo welcomed the Sixth Form class back at a special assembly in which he hammered home the necessity of "finishing the race" if we were all to get into the best possible college. "What's it all about?" he would ask rhetorically. And after meandering through a short history of Benedictine "Schools of the Lord's Service" such as ours, and discussing why Portsmouth's motto, "Veritas," was so significant, Vibes would eventually conclude that what it was all about was getting into a good college. Father Leo was not a gifted speaker, but his point was a practical one, and as the customary onslaught of classes, homework and term papers started we tried to apply ourselves for a final year.

The year got under way, and, despite the release of The Beatles' *Abbey Road* and of *Butch Cassidy and the Sundance Kid* late in September, football unexpectedly became the most exciting part of it. Our new coach, Phil Coen, had rejuvenated the team, and we completed an improbable series of come back victories. On the last weekend of the season we needed to beat St. George's for the first time in seventeen years to win the conference title.

I knew something was wrong when Coach Coen did not appear for the pre-game training meal. His assistant, Happy Boynewicz, looked stunned and drawn. Bill Crimmins was on hand as well, and after we had eaten, he stood up to speak.

"Coach Coen was looking forward to this game, and I want you to know how very proud he is of each and every one of you. But he can't be here today." Crimmins took a deep breath. "Coach Coen's daughter was killed in a car crash last night. He has requested that the game go forward, wants you to know he will be thinking of you, and asks that you go out and play the best game you can. Let's stand and say a prayer for Karen and all the Coen family."

Shaken, we did as we were asked, and then Happy Boynewicz bellowed, "Now let's get out there and be *animals*!"

We did go out and battle a much bigger team to a standstill in the first half. Bobby Portz was especially heroic. He ran a ball on an end-around to the two-yard line, but our fullback fumbled on the next play. Then Bobby made three ferocious tackles as St. George's tried to drive down the field. Each time he was crumpled on the grass yet managed to stand up and limp back to the huddle. After the third tackle he got up agonizingly slowly, clutching a cracked rib, and the ref whistled the play dead and ordered him off the field.

St. George's scored the first touchdown of the game after a long drive late in the third quarter. One of their halfbacks ran off tackle from the four yard line. I had a fleeting chance to dive for his ankles from my linebacker position but missed. They made the extra point, and both teams' defenses dug in determinedly from there. Our break came when Bryan McShane forced a St. George's fumble and recovered it at midfield with two minutes left. Mike Mooney threw for two quick first downs, and then we ran twice unproductively up the middle. On third down at the twenty Mooney faked into the line and rolled right. He found his flanker streaking for the end zone and threw a perfect spiral that hung forever in the air. At the last instant Robbie Rudd split his double coverage and made a circus catch for the touchdown. On the extra point we faked the kick and Mooney rolled right again. Rudd again found daylight, caught the ball and clutched it close. We were up 8-7, and fifty seconds later had hung on to win.

After the game the St. George's captain, Tom Campbell, came into our changing room, shook our hands and said, "We hated to lose, but if it had to happen we're glad it was today." At Bill Crimmins' suggestion, we knelt to pray again.

Why is it that those few hours are among the most vivid in my mind of all the 1960s? Perhaps because that day and the awful sadness of the Monday after when Father Damian drove us all in school buses to Karen Coen's funeral, were the last times it felt like we were all moving in the same direction .

5.

One of the criticisms of Father Hilary was that he was an outrageous snob, and it was true that he knew a good bit more than most monks about where certain people got their money. In one long-running argument in the dining hall over whether a San Francisco family had made their stash in railroads or mining, Joe Tobin had finally produced a book supporting his contention, and Father Hilary promptly employed the novel parliamentary maneuver of making him a waiter and sending him to get the soup. As soon as he was out of earshot, Father Hilary turned to us and exclaimed, "Joe can be such a name dropper!"

Some of the faculty appeared intimidated by Father Hilary. Others avoided him. Still others sought to undermine him. Once that Fall one of Hilary's monastic adversaries got a hold of a copy of *Women's Wear Daily* with a front-page photo of Amanda Burden and him emerging from Le Grenouille on East 52nd Street in Manhattan. Not normally a part of the monastery's daily reading fare, the paper was mysteriously placed on the Abbot's desk. The Abbot queried Father Hilary, who related the whole incident with mild indignation but a slight sparkle in his eye as well. "I told him I looked at it as mission work. You have to have lunch *some place,* after all."

But there was another side of Father Hilary's personality that was very pure. The week after the football season ended, for example, he came to my room, which was now just next to his, after knocking lightly on the door, and asked me to join him for a cup of tea. When I sat down he said, "I'm afraid I have some bad news. Rose died last night."

Rose was our house maid in Saint Bede's, a small, round, cheery Portugese-American woman, who was unfailingly kind-hearted. She must have surreptitiously placed hundreds of late term papers for Father Hilary's courses on the piles where he kept them in his room. She was always willing to take home sewing that she never let you pay her for. We did give her presents at Christmas and the end of the year, which Father Hilary chose and collected money for, and in return Rose felt suitably empowered to repeat whatever gossip she and the maids in other houses had heard. Part of me hoped that just once, after she had discovered the remains of one of his delicious dinner parties, Father Hilary would overhear Rose come in to empty my waste basket and whisper worriedly, "Father is drinking too much again." But she was far too discreet. And, of course, she was completely devoted to him, too.

Father Hilary asked me to organize the house to attend Rose's funeral the following morning.

The next day Rose's extended family—half the village of Portsmouth—turned out in the Abbey church. For many of them it was the only time they would ever see the place where Rose had toiled for three decades. Father Hilary knew that, he wanted to make sure they understood how highly Rose had been valued, and he wanted us to learn, if we did not know, how highly we ought to value her. Father Hilary celebrated the Mass with special solemnity. Father Andrew, looking even more haggard and sleepless than usual, assisted with the readings and led the singing. And Father Ambrose played the organ. They were the only three monks there. Seeing Father Hilary console Rose's family after the funeral made me realize how little those who considered him to be an old snob really understood.

That, of course, didn't stand in the way of his breaking in the new maid, Evelyn, the following week. He made a point of asking her to press his Saville Row clerical suits and shine his Lobb shoes—clothes he only wore when traveling away from the monastery-- and he himself was careful to walk around without his monk's habit on, clad only in his Italian silk underwear. "She has to get used to me some day," he explained ever so reasonably, "So it may as well be now. But *God*, I'm getting too old to break in a new maid." He gave her picayune jobs and critiqued her cleaning, asked her to run errands and sew pockets, all in the spirit of *Ora et labora*, but in due course Father Hilary and Evelyn became close friends.

Episodes like those raised the old riddle in my mind. Why Father Hilary had ever chosen the monastery was a mystery I couldn't figure out. I determined to ask him when the time was right. One night a week or two later we were sitting in his room talking about an underclassman whose performances was so poor that Vibes was considering suspending him. Father Hilary wanted to know what I thought.

"Hart is basically a good kid, but right now he just can't settle down and study."

"Yes, I've seen that so many times." He looked at me knowingly, and I knew he was thinking of me. "Punishing him would do no good. Some boys are just too busy growing up. I think we should tell the Headmaster that we need to give him more time. He'll grow out of it."

It was then I asked him.

"Father, forgive me if it's too personal, but would you mind telling me why you became a monk?"

Others had asked him over the years, and he had said something about coming home from a dinner party in Cambridge, and laying down on his bed, and before he went to sleep he had made up his mind. I wanted to hear for myself. I could feel him considering his answer as he looked at me for a moment. Then he said quietly, "Because I knew it was the one job I could never complete."

I guess I looked quizzical, because he soon added, "I had a very full bachelor life you know, and I was over thirty before I finally decided to come here. I don't want to shock you, but let's just say I wasn't very much different than you and your friends. And at a certain point that and everything else I was doing—even teaching at Tech—seemed so very empty. I had visited this place, and so I wrote. I didn't hear back, and so I wrote again a couple of months later. The first letter was lost in the mail. I suppose I was being tested. Anyway, the second letter got through and the then Prior asked me to come on as a postulant. At the end of that school year I packed up my apartment. My family had been surprised, and I have to say even I was having second thoughts. But as I was packing some glass I wrapped it in old copies of the Sunday *Boston Globe* I had saved, and in the travel section of one of them was an article about Fort Augustus in Scotland, where I was to be sent for my novitiate, if I got that far. I took that to be a good sign and never looked back."

"And do you feel like you have completed your monastic profession now?"

"Oh, no. Not even close. Jesus didn't call the righteous you know. And we may all be proud and sinful, but some of us got an extra dose. Jamie, I am, so very prideful, in case you haven't noticed. Like the Jews, our job here is not to change the world, but to change ourselves. The point is that I'd rather fail at being a poor excuse for a monk than succeed at anything else I might have turned my hand to." He smiled slightly, and I understood the interview to be over.

But the more I have thought about it, it was then that Father Hilary summed up the terrible yet tremendous nature of his vocation. It was not an easy choice to make. He was at some level an urban fleshpot and at another a Puritan penitent. He loved people, but he knew he had to try to love God first. He worked hard to acquire an ascetic spirituality without ever losing his sensual nature and love of beauty; and those different sides of his personality were at war in a battle from which neither side could ever claim total victory. But bravely, sometimes merrily, often grimly, he knew which side he wished to fight on. And for nearly sixty years, he tried.

You can never really know another person completely. We are all of us strangers to some degree, not only to others, but even unto ourselves. But I felt I knew Father Hilary then, however mysterious a part of him remained. And whatever his faults, I admired him deeply.

If Father Hilary didn't qualify as trying to live a committed life, then I didn't know anyone who did. And if he could make that commitment, with all of his gifts and weaknesses intermingled, I had to wonder if, or how, the rest of us could ever do the same. Wasn't that, in the end, what we were here to figure out? "What's it all about?" Father Leo would ask melodramatically in school assemblies, and we would mercilessly mimic him, of course; but that *was* the question. Father Hilary and the other monks had decided upon their answer. Somewhere, some place, at some time or another, the rest of us would have to provide ours.

6.

We were in the Abbey church again on a December Sunday morning, and my mind was wandering. The year was coming to a close. John Lennon had returned his Member of the British Empire medal to protest the British Government's involvement in the Nigerian Civil War. Black Panther members Fred Hampton and Mark Clark had been shot to death in their sleep by fourteen Chicago cops bursting into their pad. The Altamont Free Concert, hosted by the Rolling Stones as an attempt at a "Woodstock West," erupted into violence and, instead, came to be viewed as the end of the sixties.

> *Credo in unum Deum,*
> *Patrem omnipotentem, factoreum caeli et terra,*
> *Visibilium omnium, et invisibilium....*

The Creed was that part of the Mass where Catholics affirm their core beliefs, developed by the Greeks through dispute, debate and discussion in the early centuries of the Church, and included in the body of the Mass at St. Benedict's behest: That One God created everything visible and invisible, that he sent his only Son to suffer and die for our sins, who on the third day after his death rose and ascended into Heaven, where He sat at the right hand of the Father to judge the living and the dead....

It sounded preposterous on the face of it, of course, even if the Catholic Church had not yet then been in the beginning of a free fall, its bishops fumbling to figure out a way to emerge from the Inferno they and their high-priced lawyers had created, when instead of managing their seminaries and professing

Church teaching they had turned the other cheek to outright dissent, disobedience and disgusting crimes. And yet, despite how preposterous the tenets of the Creed sounded, that morning I wondered if it could not be true. And who was I to speak, anyway? My own derelictions were far too clear.

Could it be true? Yes. Could it be true to the exclusion of all other religious truth? And if one could not affirm that, did that not imply that all truth was relative, and, therefore, untrue, to one or another degree? So it would seem, and yet that morning I really wished to believe that what was in some way true could also be entirely true, at least in our limited capacity to understand Truth, or the portion of it to which we were granted access. And what a small shard of life that might be, a speck of dust among gazillions of others, sometimes lit and sometimes dark, benighted, bemused, bedeviled, but hanging in and carrying on, for some purpose, if only we could figure out what. A Mystery.

"Belief," Abbot Matthew had told us, "is the willingness, even the necessity to accept the possibility of mystery, while we are in the terrestrial order, when our minds are limited to knowledge of the finite."

Now we see as through a glass darkly, but then, face to face.
Now I know in part; then I shall understand fully even as I have been understood.

V. 1970

1.

In early January, when we straggled back from vacation for our last winter at Portsmouth, the wind was fierce and the whole campus frozen. As I struggled through the snow with my suitcase up the icy footpath to St. Bede's, the wet cold began to seep through my weathered Wallabys into my socks, and a full comprehension of the three long months that lay ahead descended like a dense, dark cloud.

I opened the door to Saint Bede's and flicked on the hallway lights. They shone down into floors so heavily waxed in our absence that I could see my reflection looking up at me. The wax odor was rich and somewhat sweet, positively sensual compared to the scarred, scruffy, dank smelling quarters we had departed before Christmas.

It would only last a day or so, but I savored the moment. I could tell Father Hilary I was back, but there was no rush. Tomorrow morning the bells would ring long before the gray, bitter cold dawn. The peace and quiet and the scent of wax would be as inexorably gone as last spring's blossoms on the Japanese cherry tree outside Father Hilary's door. Soon enough Saint Bede's would be crowded with the conflicts and confusions of thirty teenagers. Now it was, soothingly, silent.

I got to my room, turned on the light and threw my suitcase on a chair. I looked out the window that faced Narragansett Bay. Even in night-time when the water could be more sensed than seen, it was a welcome view. A thick sheet of ice had formed on the window, however, and would probably not thaw until March. It was already the dead of winter.

There was a knock on my door, and I yelled, "Come in." The door opened slowly, and that unmistakable voice breathed, "*Excuse* me."

I bolted up and stammered, "Good evening, Father."

Father Hilary was leaning forward slightly, a mischevious grin on his face.

"Isn't it customary to greet one's housemaster upon arrival returning from vacation?"

"Yes, Father."

"I thought so, but I wasn't sure, so I thought I had better check with a prefect. They're supposed to know the rules, you see."

He was speaking drily, but his eyes sparkled.

"I'm sorry, Father. I was about to come in."

"Good. Tommy just arrived. We're having a cup of tea. Come join us."

He bowed slightly and exited backwards.

When I got there, Tommy was wolfing down a pastry, Father Hilary was playing Debussy on his stereo and talking about Norman Mailer's *Armies of the Night*. Tommy excused himself at the earliest possible moment, saying he had some studying to do.

"How very conscientious!" Father Hilary exclaimed. He knew from long experience that on the first night back from a vacation schoolboys concentrated their energies on bullshitting each other to death and would never dream of cracking a book. But he let Tommy go. After the door closed Father Hilary gave it a lifted eyebrow and began a discussion of the *trecento* paintings he had recently seen at the Fogg Museum, including a recently restored Duccio of the Annunciation. "I'd forgotten how beautiful it was," he said, as if speaking of an old friend before he looked at his watch. "Well, maybe you better get some studying in as well."

I stopped by Tommy's room. He had his headphones on, but the music was turned up so loudly I could hear "Uncle John's Band" from the Grateful Dead album *Workingman's Dead*. He had turned on his black light so his Peter Max posters glowed, and he had donned dark glasses to shield his eyes.

By the end of the Fall term our records were complete so far as what the colleges we might want to go to would see, and this made coming back to Portsmouth in the depths of January feel all the more futile. That last Winter term began slowly. Father Leo was the one person who resisted the general lethargy. He plowed through mountains of paper work and attended to a Herculean number of other administrative tasks, all the while exhorting the rest of us to "finish the race." He had an infinite capacity for hard work and a deficit in the requirements for human relations and humor. Thus, he was less than appreciative when Bob Rambusch, recalling Father Leo's work at Los Alamos, scotch taped a photo of the Hiroshima bombing onto his prayer carrel in the chapel. Nor did he approve when Michael Garvey stuffed a paper napkin into the bell he banged with his open palm for silence so that he could deliver after lunch announcements. He hit the thing so often and so hard before he figured out the prank that he bloodied his palm, a partial stigmata. A couple of weeks later Father Leo was halfway through reading an editorial to a school assembly from the *Deerfield Scroll* entitled "Let's Keep Off the Grass," before the rising tide of laughter from even the lower forms present alerted him to the fact that authors had a double meaning in mind, and were not soley interested in campus beautification. Vibes persevered until he got to the line, "Furthermore, the grass is at its greenest in spring, so we must take care to exercise the necessary restraint now if we are to enjoy its fruits to the fullest then." Another loud guffaw rippled through the crowd, and Father Leo looked up, and slowly his face became plastered with a monumental shit-eating grin. He walked out in embarrassment.

The auditorium broke into an uproar of hilarity, and then at once became utterly still. Father Andrew had been skulking, as he so often did, as a self-appointed monitor in chapel and at assemblies, and now he stepped out of the shadows and stood upon the stage Vibes had just so ignominiously departed. Boys' antennae being ever alert to anarchic impulses, we knew they had clashed occasionally. Several weeks before Father Leo had changed his physics class schedule and Father Andrew had yelled at him in public for doing so without getting his permission. "I knew it would come to this,"

Father Leo had replied, "That one day the Headmaster would be accused of running the School."

It was the funniest line we had ever heard him utter, but that was an eternity ago. Now Father Andrew spoke quietly, yet his resonant voice carried into the bones of every boy in the room.

> "How many times in our lives have we made mistakes, even foolish mistakes, and how would we like to be treated when we did? With mockery or with compassion, even sympathy, born out of our knowledge of human failing?"

Father Andrew spoke without anger, and that made his reproach cut all the more deeply.

"As you leave tonight, you might take a moment to reflect upon the Golden Rule and remember: no matter how bright you think you are, kindness is never out of season."

That February Black Sabbath released the first heavy metal album, and The Who recorded "Live at Leeds," prior to their rock opera "Tommy" premiering at the Metropolitan Opera that spring. Within a couple of months Paul McCartney had left The Beatles and the *Elton John* album was released.

That winter Father Hilary took us on trips to the Frick Museum in New York to see Bellini's St. Francis, the Holbeins of Thomas More and Thomas Cromwell, and the El Greco of Saint Jerome. He took us to the Gardner Museum in Boston to view the Gorgiones and Veronese, to hear chamber music in the sort of setting for which it had been composed, and to experience the sensual delight of walking upon so much Carrera marble. We went to the National Gallery in Washington to see the Leonardos and so many other masterpieces. The director, John Walker, was an old friend of Father Hilary's and walked us through the Italian rooms, until his handsome young assistant in a bespoke Saville Row suit, Carter Brown, arrived and called him away to a meeting. "I'm afraid I need to have a word with Hamlet about an upcoming exhibition," he explained to Father Hilary as he shook his hand goodbye. We of course continued, and all along the way Father Hilary drove his points home. How Cimbue's *Virgin* "in softer lines," revolutionary in the 13th century, was carried through the streets of Florence in triumphal procession from the painter's house to the church of Santa Maria Novella for which it had been commissioned. How Giotto had taken the next step of painting what Vasari called the true human form. Father Hilary, however, always emphasized the importance these early Renaissance artists placed on having true faith and strict morals.

> "They believed that virtue was inseparable from good art and took for granted that a work revealed the artist's soul as well as his mind. As time went on secular subjects gained in importance, in part because of a new technique: painting on canvas with pigments carried in oils. Michelangelo scorned this new trick 'fit only for women and children,' because the inept could so easily correct a mistake by scraping it off and trying again. Before oils, you see, pigments dissolved in pure or lime water were applied to a wall which the artist himself had plastered; or the colors were mixed with egg yolk and water, to a panel of

poplar wood. To paint one must have had an infallible hand and a far-seeing mind; each stroke was final, as in a water color today. And yet, even as the secular crept into the traditions of sacred art, for several hundred years more the ideas of order and ethics remained in place, until the nervous rhythms of the 20th century began to drive us in a new direction."

Back at the School, Father Andrew had been up for weeks working around the clock trying, in those pre-computer days, to formulate a schedule that would put each of the school's 220 boys in precisely the right class and just the right section each of the six periods of the day. He had worked himself into a kind of frenzied catatonia, swearing and spluttering. He achieved this rarefied state several times a year until Hilary would take him aside, cook him a hot meal and gently upbraid him. "When you do this to yourself," Father Hilary would say, "You pervert your virtues into vices and so diminish us all." Then he'd send Andrew off to bed, wherever that was.

Not long after Father Hilary caught one of his habitual nasty colds and became bedridden as well. Now Father Andrew heard of Hilary's distress and determined to come to his aid. He abandoned his slide rule and rubble strewn rat's nest of an office and made up a tray of supper from the kitchen to carry down to Father Hilary's room. It was February by now, the heart of Rhode Island's winter, and a blizzard was raging. Father Andrew had discarded his hood and scapular and was fighting his way through the storm in his threadbare black habit, the ancient black loafers he wore on his feet having by now more holes than leather. He waded through the snow, leaning against the wind, finally reached Father Hilary's outer door and knocked. I heard what happened next from my room next door.

From within came Father Hilary's muffled groan, "Go away."

Sure there was a misunderstanding, Father Andrew called out, "It's me, Andrew."

"I don't care. Go away."

"You're a sick man, Father. I've brought you some supper."

"I don't want it. Leave me alone."

Fraternal dialogue ended at that point. Father Andrew ripped the door open with one hand, and with the other threw the tray across the room so that it crashed into the far wall, where the remains of the lemon meringue pie stuck to Father Hilary's prized

Picasso drawing. Then Andrew stalked off into the night, cursing like a sailor, leaving the door wide open as the wind roared and snow began to gather on the edge of Father Hilary's rug.

When I related this episode from *The Lives of the Saints* to Bill Crimmins he roared with laughter, but then looked at me earnestly and said, "You must promise never to repeat that story."

"Never?"

"Not while either of them is still alive. It would give people the wrong idea."

"That monks can be difficult and irrational like the rest of us?"

"Of course, they can be. And no two more than Hilary and Andrew. But they're so much more than that, too. When I was a boy here the war was on, and I lost my oldest brother when the Canadian

Royal Air Force plane he was piloting was shot down over France on D-Day. A year later I was called to the Headmaster's room about nine o'clock at night for milk and cookies. My other brother had been killed fighting for the Marines on Okinawa. My one privilege was to say I needn't go back to study hall.

"I was angry as hell and began walking up and down the Monk's Walk, that alley of oaks parallel to the main driveway, with my fists clenched. I was fifteen years old and wanted to kill every Jap and German in the world. There was no moon in the sky, and only an odd star, so it was very dark. I began shouting at the gods, my voice dissolving into the heavens, muffled by the roar of the winds in the branches above. I walked and walked and around eleven I suppose it was, I sensed that someone was walking with me. It was Andrew. He never spoke. He knew there was nothing he nor anybody else could say, but he just walked beside me, until by about one in the morning I had walked myself out and could go to bed.

"St. Thomas a Kempis once said, 'I would rather feel compassion than know its definition.' Andrew is the epitome of compassion and certainly knows its definition."

Bill Crimmins was looking at me with kind and penetrating eyes, and I knew what he was saying was true.

2.

Sursum corda
Habemus ad Dominum
Gratias acamus Domino Deo nostro
Dignum et iustum est

Lift up your hearts. Lift them up to the Lord. What a very strange concept. It had been so long since I had ever imagined doing such a thing. But the idea had its appeal, on a somber Sunday in the church, whether it was to God or somewhere else. It was hard to live without faith and hope, no matter that so many of the world's smart guys in the past two hundred years had insisted that was the only option. It sounded kind of cool, but in practice it wasn't always quite as cool as it sounded. I had learned that the hard way.

Winter moved along with glacial speed. Finally, around the end of February, there were a few days of cloud-dappled but mostly clear blue evening skies in which one could sense at last that winter might some day end. Winter was breaking up, although Spring was far from ready to arrive. It was a time to watch and wait.

That term we read Arthur Koestler's *Darkness at Noon*. Rubashov's dilemma resonated in our heads. Did the ends justify the means? To advance the purposes of the State? No, we answered with confidence. Could they ever? No. The western moral teaching was clear on that point.

But Koestler seemed to have Plato, Aristotle and a whole range of Christian teaching on his side as well. It was a strong case, even if it caused problems for The Chicago Seven and SDS. The Revolution might come, but only if it did so morally. Was that feasible? The Russian Communists hadn't thought so. Should we?

We had grown pretty disillusioned with politics. When Nixon had greeted over a million anti-war protesters at the Moratorium in November by proclaiming it was a great day for football, that kind of summed things up.

But if we students were such pure adherents of revolutionary utopianism, why were a bunch of jerks stealing cigarettes out of Father Hilary's vase? If we believed in peace so much, why did we get so much pleasure out of busting up an opposing athlete on the football field?

Some questions had no good answers.

3.

In mid-March Tommy and I visited Porter. Spring vacation had begun. His family lived in an old neighborhood south of Miami called Coconut Grove, full of ancient palm trees, bamboo, bromeliads and blossoming vines. Settlers by the shore had lived in shelters of palmetto leaves thatched on wooden frames here early in the 20th century. They had fished the local waters, cooking loggerhead turtle steaks, crawfish and the occasional chicken outdoors over a chip fire. Half a century later, the Carrolls lived in an airy, rambling, Spanish-style house with a long lawn that ended at a mangrove swamp, beyond which one could see to

Biscayne Bay. There were ironwood, gumbo limbo and straggler fig trees still in the Grove, as well as the poisonous machineel, that was said to have sent men who axed it falling to their knees, heads reeling and faces swelling in the tropical sun. At night the wind blew benignly through the palms and the moist air rustled the dense fronds, making a noise at once dramatic and soothing as we sat on the screened porch looking down towards the water.

At Coral Gables High Porter had been placed entirely in AP courses and said the homework, when assigned, took twenty minutes to complete. "Up there they treated me like a moron, and here it's all *tranquilo*," he mused as we sipped beers, the humidity of the March breeze washing over us like a cure.

Porter was formally in school the first few days we were there, but he was always back at the house by noon, which was about the time we woke up. His parents were remarkably tolerant of the adolescent genius for just hanging around, and we lounged by the pool by the hour, interrupted only by an occasional refrigerator raid. Occasionally Anne, Porter's sister, now a pretty junior at Concord Academy with budding crab apple breasts and a flashing smile, would sit with us and trade sarcasms about boarding school life. Porter did not hesitate to tell her to get lost when he wanted to hit up some reefer or do anything, for that matter, that transcended what he took to be her limited capability for coolness. When we were told to go to Mass the first Sunday, Porter bought the Sunday newspapers on the way, and we read them in the parking lot at St. Hugh's church. When Anne objected, he snorted, "If you think it's so important you can go in there." She glared at him and promptly did. I liked her for that show of spirit.

Porter had lost no time acquiring a hot-blooded Cuban girlfriend named Miranda, and one afternoon we went speedboating into the Everglades with her sister Carmen and her. Miranda wore a Navajo headband. She swore every time Porter hit a bump, which provoked him to do so as often as possible. BUMP.

They were obviously in love.

 "Just like a Willys in four-wheel drive," Porter sang from the Dead's "Sugar Magnolia" over and over as she berated him. What more amorous metaphor could be conceived than comparing your woman to a jeep?

We survived the boat ride and spent the remaining days sunning ourselves, going to movies, drinking "blend" at Gil's Spot, a local black bar, and satiating late night munchies at the Dollar Pancake House on Dixie Highway.

On the final days of the vacation Father Hilary came through Miami for a Portsmouth fund raising and school promotion trip. Porter's parents had sportingly committed to hosting a dinner for the cause. Father Hilary Hilary came downstairs that evening wearing a white silk jacket with a black kerchief. He looked like a refugee from *Casablanca* and charmed the pants off the lady next to him with stories about the Duke and Duchess of

Windsor not paying their bills, and what had *really* gone on when he had been asked to give Catholic instruction to Jackie Kennedy's half-sister Janet Auchincloss in the Camelot White House prior to her marriage to Lewis Rutherfurd. At the end of the evening his dinner partner kissed him on the cheek and gushed, "I'm so glad to have met you. Dotty told me I was going to be sitting next to some old monk."

4.

That Spring Term began in Holy Week. As soon as we got back to school we began our Easter Retreat. The visiting retreat master was a swarthy but soft-spoken Dominican, who tried to appeal to our intellects, but lost his audience early when he read a line of his own poetry on the death of Albert Camus: "When your car kissed that tree…"

A reasoned and compassionate defense of the church's moral teaching might have eventually alienated a bunch of disillusioned adolescents, but he did it quickly with one line of mediocre poetry.

After Mass and the Washing of the Feet on Holy Thursday evening Tommy and I had signed up for The Vigil between one and two in the morning. Once we got to the chapel I tried to be vigilant but fell asleep after thirty minutes. When I woke Father Andrew was holding my arm and whispering, "Come on, sit up. If you want to go to bed you can, but please sit up if you're going to stay."

On Good Friday we prayed the Passion. Some of the monks looked as if they had taken their Lenten fasting to an extreme. Father Ambrose's wan face, in particular, looked like wax in the candlelight, and I couldn't help but wonder if the redemptive power of abstinence would ever make sense to any of us.

We were supposed to spend Holy Saturday in quiet reflection. "Look beyond the symbols," our retreat master pleaded with us in his noontime conference, "and the petty little rules, and all the other things you find so easy to resent, and try to see what the deeper truth is, what the ultimate reality of Jesus' death and resurrection, of God's intervention into human history, really means for you and for all of us."

The sound of snoring came from the back of the church. The Retreat Master called us to our knees, we said a perfunctory Hail Mary, and he dismissed us. After lunch word got around that someone had acid, and a bunch of people were going to go down to the woods to drop it. I was still sleepy from the night before and had begun to wonder if I hadn't done enough LSD for one lifetime, so I wandered into the house library and pulled down a collection of Bertrand Russell's essays.

> "I am quite confident that a system of morals and ethics could be constructed without reference to a higher being."

Then why didn't he do it? I stared out at the early signs of spring—forsythia blooming, cherry trees in bloom, the other, older trees just beginning to bud—and thought of all the religion they had tried to teach us at Portsmouth. The Benedictines prided themselves on a catholic with a small "c" approach to teaching Christian Doctrine, and over the years we had read broadly in many religious and philosophical traditions. Who was this noisy preacher in the Palestine of Princeps Augustus and Tiberius, full of imprecations and ambiguities, audaciously promising to illumine our lives on earth and forever afterward? The Son of Man? It sounded highly improbable.

Schopenhauer fit my mood much better. Real happiness was impossible. Existence itself was a crime. Those were sentiments Tommy and I had harbored for some time. The Stoics were the most approachable. Nature would unfold somehow, Epictetus taught, and what was important was the attitude you took to it—sober and ethical-- not the events themselves. But Epicurus was on the money too. Have a good time, keep life simple and abstain from evil doing. J.S. Mills' elevation of Epicureanism to Utilitarianism, doing that which gave the greatest good to the largest cross section of society, sounded a tad idealistic. It also sounded hard. I preferred the Existential approach—the repudiation of any systematic, organized view of the world in favor of a consciousness that just goes along. Following any other path, from the Nichomachean Ethic to Thomas Aquinas, involved too much work. It was better to slag. I therefore took a nap and thus missed a great adventure.

The other guys did indeed drop acid. They were down by the water when the drug began to take hold, and as the blood began to beat harder inside their heads they began to rove the shore. Someone discovered a clump of newly budding berry bushes, and soon they had all stripped off their shirts and were applying war paint. All that remained was for a suitable adversary to come along, and around five o'clock it did.

The twice-weekly freight train from Providence to Newport ran on an old line of tracks down by the

Bay. As it approached the school property it slowed because the line was old, and boys making fires in the woods had resorted to removing railroad ties for fuel, reducing the stability of the rails. The Indian trippers suddenly descended, whooping up a storm, running for the train. To their surprise the Engineer stopped the train, climbed down with a crow- bar and dispersed the attackers in short order. Then he used his two-way radio to call the police, who reported the incident to Father Leo, and all hell broke loose. The students involved were rounded up and questioned sternly by detectives, while the final conference of the Easter Retreat went on.

That night the Easter Mass began outside the church, as candles were lit from a charcoal grill that, aside from this annual liturgical purpose, was normally reserved for carbonizing the monks' hot dogs during summer cook outs. The previous year someone had surreptitiously doused the charcoal with water so it would not light, and to prevent a repeat of that catastrophe a slightly nerdy looking novice had stood nervously by the grill all afternoon. But Chris Buckley and Allan Docal had persuaded an underformer to distract the young monk long enough for them to embed M-80s deep in the charcoal and pour gasoline over it. Thus, when Vibes lit the fire late that evening it soared gratifyingly high up into the sky, leaving a spume not unlike Hiroshima's.

We shuffled into the darkened chapel behind the Abbot, bearing the New Light of the World, the sound of fireworks exploding behind us. The chapel creaked and groaned in the stiff spring wind

as slowly the candles filled it with light and the service began. The
Indians had returned among us from their interrogation. They were freshly bathed and looked chastened, dazed or faintly ill.

The Mass went forward magnificently, whether one thought it meant anything or not. And Father Hilary provided the sermon, emphasizing at first, "We *are* our brothers' keepers." It struck as something he might have been reminding himself of rather too often those days. Then he started on another tack.

"What use are we to make, this Easter night, of God's creatures? Before we say any thing we must begin with a friendly feeling towards our fellow creatures; they are meant to be there; they have undergone a Heavenly scrutiny and have been declared very good. There can be no question that the attitude of Saint Francis of Assisi is the right attitude. His childlike acceptance of all created things, and the welcome he extended to them as his brothers and sisters was correct.

"Our use of creatures in the widest sense, that is, of all the material blessings God gives us—food, warmth, exercise, work, recreation, amusements, leisure, friendships, and so on, is of the greatest possible importance in our spiritual lives. For, after all, we have got to use creatures, and we have got to decide *how* to use them. Even a hermit on top of a pillar has to decide whether to stand facing the wind or with his back to it. We are making use of God's creatures all day, and night comes, and we make use of His gift of sleep.

"Our use of creatures must be an art. Let us think of man's life as a voyage by ship. He has a supernatural harbor to reach, and the accomplishment of that journey is his principal care, a case beside which all others shrink into insignificance. Yet he has to take supplies on board; his fellow creatures are to be his fellow passengers on the voyage. It is evident that the captain of the ship must apportion his supplies with a view to sailing efficiently. Prudence must determine how much use of creatures we are to allow ourselves. In a fallen world like ours, we have to fear the waves and storms we shall encounter. Let us take stock, then, of the supplies we mean to carry."

I didn't understand all of what he was saying but was struck by the fact that it was as if Father Hilary could read our minds. A hermit on a pillar. That sort of summed me up. And which way was I going to bend?

After the Mass there was a celebration in the dining room with lots of cocoa and cookies to take the chill off the deep night. When we got back to Saint Bede's Father Hilary was cooking a late supper for the Crimmins, the Scottis and some other old friends who had come out to the Abbey for midnight Mass. They were eating and drinking, and Father Hilary had left his door to the rest of the house open to let smoke ventilate when we heard his slightly looped voice ring out, "*I don't believe in God half the time, but that's beside the point*!"

There was heated argument thereafter and the sounds of champagne glasses clicking, so we took the opportunity to organize a track meet on the rectangular roof of St. Bede's, sprinting around corners until our legs splayed beneath the starriest of skies in which the Lord in Whom Father Hilary had said he did not always believe, but to Whom he had devoted his life, had Risen, however tentatively, into the heavens above southern Rhode Island.

5.

The following week we registered for the draft. The local Selective Service Center had sent all seniors letters with questionnaires so that they could assign us a classification. Anyone going to college would qualify for a deferral, of course. But there was no guarantee that hostilities in Southeast Asia would not escalate. Most of us applied for our 2S deferral. A couple of guys claimed Conscientious Objector status. I wrote a postscript on my 2S application that if it were ever changed I would claim CO status. I wanted them to know that I was an idealist at heart.

It may not have mattered very much. Troop levels, which had reached a maximum of 530,000 in 1969, were declining. By the end of 1970 they would fall below 400,000. Fewer people were being drafted every year. But it was impossible to know what to believe. We had been lied to too often about Vietnam, from JFK to LBJ to Tricky Dick, and still to come were among the most vicious lies, including Henry Kissinger's election eve proclamation in 1972: "Peace is at hand."

Suddenly, something was wrong with Tommy. He was completely listless and detached. "Let's take a walk," I suggested, and he got off of his bed and put on his shoes. We headed up the lane and out into the quiet cow pastures, now once more growing green. There was the perfume of fruit blossoms and newly mown grass in the air. The azalea were starting to flame, and soon the large rhododendron bushes would follow. It was the best time of year, or should have been.

I had tried to make some small talk when we started walking, but I soon gave up and communed with Tommy in his gloomy silence. Then he sighed, "It just doesn't make any sense."

"Are you feeling OK?"

"I'm not sick, if that's what you mean. I just can't make it anymore."

We came back to the house. I told Father Hilary I thought Tommy needed some help. His response was neutral and monosyllabic, so I went into my room and resumed reading *King Lear*:

> *... Come,*
> *Let's away to prison.*
> *We two alone will sing like birds in the cage,*

> *When thou dost ask me blessing, I'll kneel down*
> *And ask of thee forgiveness,*
>
> *And so we'll live, and pray and sing....*
> *...and take upon us*
> *The mystery of things, as if we were God's spies.*

Is that what you were supposed to do in a monastery?

Later, Father Hilary knocked on my door and invited me into tea. "You look a little peaked tonight," he said, "Try this," and poured a dollop of the Chivas Regal we had given him for Christmas into my tea. "They're both woody flavors and go together well." Then he talked about Tommy.

"I knew as soon as I saw him that he had to get away from here, and the Headmaster agreed with me…eventually."

He rolled his eyes ever so slightly and then leaned forward.

"Tommy is on his way home for a few days. His mother will see that he gets some rest and professional counseling. I expect when he comes back, he will be completely himself again.

"The way I feel about these situations is that sensitivity is a double-edged sword, and some times it can be Hell to live with, and one suffers. But in the end, it's worth it."

He was looking right at me, and I knew that every episode I had been through at Portsmouth—whether studies, depression, sexual uncertainty or drugs—he had already seen it and understood. We were growing up in fits and starts, and with more than our share of stumbles, and Father Hilary seemed to understand that. Each of us had his creatures to contend with, and I realized that Father Hilary himself must have had more than most. He sent me back to my room then, and though we were to have pain aplenty in the last few weeks of the year, I never stopped feeling close to him. And I knew, however much I would provoke him, he never stopped caring for me.

6.

I spent a lot of time in those last weeks at Portsmouth closeted in a rehearsal room beneath the auditorium, playing the piano. Father Ambrose looked in encouragingly from time to time. When I confided the troubles I was facing to him, Ambrose looked at me sympathetically, "You know, the real problem is that you've outgrown this place. It's time to move on. But remember to take music with you. The day will come when you come home at night and don't want to rush outside to play baseball."

When college admissions came in I did better than I deserved: Johns Hopkins.

The First International Student Conference on Drug Education was on the last weekend in April. It was a student council affair in which schools from all over the East sent representatives to meet in the convention hall of a New York hotel. There was room for another delegate, and I suggested to the headmaster that going to the conference might do an underformer named Catesby Campion some good, whose parents, I knew, had a big apartment nearby. Father Leo had been reluctant to let me go but nodded his head vigorously. "Good idea. He could profit from some education on that subject."

Catesby acted incredibly cheerful at the prospect of going to New York, and no sooner had we walked out the school gates than I found out why. Walking up the lane to catch the bus to the Providence train station, he produced a vial and withdrew two pills from it.

"What's that?"

"Two hits of sunshine. This is too perfect."

"What do you mean?"

"We can't possibly go to a conference on drugs straight. That would be a contradiction in terms. Besides, we're off school property."

His logic was unassailable. We each took a tab of acid without thinking more about it
By the time we had gotten to New London, however, we were thinking about it a good deal, and by the time we got to New Haven, where the Bobby Seale trial was in progress and helicopters were

circling the city making a deafening noise, our thoughts were ricocheting off one another a billion times faster than we could hope to describe them. By the time we pulled into New York City we were hardly thinking at all. We took the subway uptown to drop our bags at Catesby's parents' pad on Park Avenue and immediately headed for the Village, where we wandered around Bleeker Street until we stumbled into the latest Godard movie, *Two Plus Two/ Sympathy for the Devil.*

By now we were at the far perimeter of the outermost mental spaces, and the juxtaposition on screen of Black Maoists standing on top of junk piles reading radical polemics with Mick Jagger trying to get it right at a recording session was enough to blow what was left of both of our minds. When we came out we ended up in Washington

Square Park where Catesby felt the need to lay down on his stomach and examine a single blade of grass with utter concentration until the first shards of light began to fleck the Manhattan sky.

"Let's go."

"I can't."

We slept most of the next day. I felt wasted but knew we had to make an appearance at the conference, so I struggled down to the Roosevelt Hotel and registered us. I actually sat in the hall for a couple of hours, although jagged as I was it was difficult to take much in. In the days ahead I decided that, however much fun recreational drugs might be for some people, I never wanted to do them again.

7.

The next weekend was the Prom, the social highlight of the Portsmouth year. I loathed the whole idea. Possibly this had to do with the fact that the two girls I had invited had both said no. But no matter. If everyone else wanted to go in for obsolete and superficial modalities of repressed social interaction they could. I was going to do something more meaningful and read *The Harrad Experiment*.

I watched testily as the girls began arriving on Friday evening, until I couldn't take it any longer and went for a long walk in the woods, built a fire and stared deep into the flames. There was an informal dance on Friday night in the auditorium, and the sound of the soul music the DJ was playing carried down to the shore. I could have had a reasonably good time going up there and hanging out if I had let myself, but it was too late for that. I had made up my mind and would just tough it out. Eventually I made my way back to Saint Bede's and a fitful sleep.

The next day was a rainy, cold, wet miserable Rhode Island morning which in due course turned into a cold wet miserable Rhode Island afternoon. I was lying on my bed, listening to the Grateful Dead:

> *"Driving that train,*
> *High on cocaine,*
> *Casey Jones you better*
> *Watch your speed.*
>
> *Trouble ahead, trouble behind..."*

Anne Carroll had come from Concord on a blind date that had not gone well. She knocked on my window and said, "That guy is such a dork. Shall we go for a walk?"

We headed down towards the Bay. A high-pressure front had blown in after the rain, and the stars were out as bright as I had ever seen them. We were stunned by the startling silence of the star-filled sky.

"It goes on forever," I said.

"Which one is that?" asked Anne, pointing upwards.

"Andromeda."

We both swung around to see who had spoken. Father Andrew came out of the shadows and said, "It's beautiful tonight, isn't it? The spring sky is always so full of surprises up here." Then he sprang off in the direction of the monastery and left us to ourselves.

8.

The next night, as every Sunday, we went to Benediction and then heard the monks sing Compline, the ancient night prayer of the Church:

> *Procul recedant somnia*
> *Et noctum phantasmata*
> *Hostemque nostrum comprime*
> *Ne polluantur corpora*

How the Hell, I wondered, was I supposed to "put evil dreams to flight with all the Phantoms of the night" and secure a holy rest for Tommy, who had indeed returned to school with his spirits restored after his brief break, or any of the rest of us?

After a quick supper I went into my rehearsal room and worked on Bach. It had a mathematical glory to it that, had I any more talent for math than I did for the piano, I'm sure I would have loved unraveling. But just playing the pieces calmed the storms within and gave me a glimpse of peace. When I emerged the air was fragrant with the scent of Spring. The change to daylight savings had occurred a couple of weeks before, and over Prom weekend the blossoms had unfolded from all the trees. Spring, soft spring, was in the air, and the sky was still blue and the grass a deep green.

Yet inside I felt totally numb.

I got back to Saint Bede's in time for study hall. I sat in my room and tried to study. We all seemed poisoned and corrupted to me, then, and I couldn't figure out how to get unpoisoned.

It was Spring, and it hurt.

9.

The year was drawing to a close, and the fractured feeling of the time and place never really shifted for the better. If anything, the outer world began to manifest the same hostility and violence we had experienced in our little lives along the Narragansett Bay. One morning at breakfast in mid-May the paper's headline blared:

National Guard Fires on Student Protest in Ohio: Four Dead.

It was a moment when you felt like you'd been kicked right through the stomach, and all you really wanted to do was to crawl away and die. The dining room was unusually hushed, even for breakfast, when Vibes rose to say the closing prayer. "It's a terrible tragedy; we must pray for all concerned." Our History AP teacher, Jim Garman, said in class that morning, "It was bound to happen sooner or later." Bound to happen? Why was it bound to happen?

The Beatles released their twelfth and final album, *Let It Be*, that May, and the New York Knick won their first NBA championship against the Lakers at Madison Square Garden, but neither of those things really helped.

Abbot Matthew's answer to the times was stark. His turn to preach again came around on the last Sunday of the year, the very morning of Commencement.

"If there is no God then what is the source of meaning in our lives? And especially, what is the source of our ethical and moral values? Is it the law? If something is legal is it therefore moral? Legality derives from a mere consensus of opinion. If you ask someone why the government ought not to torture people the answer is given, 'You wouldn't want someone to do that to you, so it shouldn't be done to someone else.'

"But this raises a question: 'Why not?' The Pope says capital punishment is an offense against humanity. I can agree with him as speaking on behalf of Christ, but apart from the teaching of the Gospel, I see no reason for not killing off murderers and rapists. What's the difference between them and a mad dog? We go around and around without admitting the existence of a God who determines right and wrong, and Who will judge us by His standard.

"Of course, it may be put that this is no real proof of God's existence; there may be no God, just a society that formulates laws that make living together bearable. Man may be an accident on the face of the earth, good or bad as you like. Such a view, however, assumes there is no right and wrong, and therefore the rules of the game can change at will; and thus there was nothing wrong with Hitler or whomever else is exerting power. Talk about human rights is nonsense in this case because the only rights a people have are those the empowered wish to give them.

"But if there is a God who cares for mankind and Who Himself is good and knows no evil, then there may well be human rights, but there will also be wrongs that we do, and we may be accountable for them. I think the rejection of God may be largely based on the desire to avoid that accountability.

"I suspect that our society is a very fragile one, and we are living off the past values of a Christian and Jewish religious heritage, without accepting or acknowledging the source of those values, and without owning up to our own responsibilities to them.

"If Christianity and the Catholic Church in particular are not the truth, there is absolutely no reason for this school to exist. On the one hand students are being taught a lot of nonsense about a non-existent or highly problematic God when they should be studying something utilitarian. They are being filled with unhealthy scruples against sex, common sense in business, and so forth in the name of an outdated and obscurantist religious system that deserves to disappear from the face of the earth. If Portsmouth is worth having around there must be a true Catholic religion to back it up; otherwise it makes no sense and should stop taking up people's lives and money."

The Abbot finished without a flourish, returned to his choir stall and sat down. There was a look of puzzlement from the parents who had come up for graduation and something close to shock among the lay faculty and monks.

To the rest of us, however—the students—what he said made a lot of sense. We knew he was talking directly to us, that he was deadly serious, and that, like it or not, we had just heard his diagnosis of the wretched excess (or was it the excessive wretchedness?) of the age. But that didn't mean we accepted or had learned the message he was trying to transmit. Instead, you could almost say, with Carl Jung, whom we had so idolized, we had opted for something more like its shadow.

At Commencement later that morning Father Leo omitted his customary thanks to the Student Council. Our valedictorian, Michael Garvey, began his address, "We have failed," and expanded on his theme persuasively.

10.

You might think that out of all these experiences—the good ones as well as the bad—might have come the beginnings of wisdom, the ability to sift through systematically, analyze what had been, and see where to head next. But it didn't work out that way. Not for me anyway.

Tommy and I were lying on the lawn at Dumbarton Oaks one hot DC day early that summer, and after a long silence he added, "I've thought of postponing college so that I can go to the International Zen Center in Switzerland and get into it all more deeply."

"Really?"

"Yeah, it just seems like we're all trying to go too fast. Everyone is living like we're running out of time. And I want to oppose that."

"Sort of like joining a monastery, isn't it?"

I had read learned or simply smart ass articles in newspapers and magazines saying, on the one hand, that we were right to be radical in the Sixties because there were horrific societal injustices that needed to be redressed; and we had to overthrow an oppressive power structure so as to create an idyllic new order. On the other hand, there were articles that said we were spoiled schmucks in the Sixties, subverting an Establishment that had created unparalleled prosperity and opportunity for those who flocked to Freedom's shores. We were self-indulgent, narcissistic, and so forth.

And you know what? They were both right. It wasn't worth bickering over anymore. There were more important things to deal with in the future than in the past, and it was time to move forward.

The existential stance I had been attracted felt oddly empty now, with an endless war in progress against an often-invisible enemy and a society whose structures—material and spiritual-- were increasingly bedeviled from within. Instead, I had new sympathy for a fourteen-hundred year old way of life a few men and women were still willing to surrender themselves to, to follow lives of obedience, poverty and prayer. It occurred to me then that what monks do is not merely admirable, but crucial to the life of the Church and society as a whole. A monk or nun who attends his vocation provides provides *all* of us an example. And that is is what Hilary, Andrew, Leo, Ambrose, Julian and the others at Portsmouth—eccentric, odd, conflicted, deeply flawed, devoted and amazingly generous as they were—had staked their lives on doing.

And how could I not try to take those examples into account as I tried to figure out my own path?

I thought of Father Damian reciting the motto of Monte Cassino: "*Succisa, virescit.*" "When cut down, it will revive and flourish." I didn't know how, and I didn't know when; but I suspected this was so. I wasn't sure of what someone like me, who could never take a vow of celibacy, or anything else, was supposed to do about it.

And yet, I knew something was there.

VI. Epilogue: Summer 1970

We flew into Duluth late one afternoon, and a bus drove fifty of us up toward Ely and the Boundary Waters. I sat next to a Black guy from Newark who had come as an alternative to serving a prison stretch. "So many trees," he repeated over and over, as we plowed down the ribbon of highway, surrounded by the infinite pine forests. I knew what he meant. I had read about wilderness schools in a magazine article and written away for Outward Bound's brochure. The pictures and descriptions had made it sound sensational to someone who had seldom been much farther into the country than the cow pastures at Portsmouth, but now I wasn't sure.

The bus broke down, and it wasn't until two in the morning that we got to our tents at the main encampment. We were up at dawn to "wild walk"—jogging through woods, wading through swamps, crossing rapids in a human chain. We came back exhausted and covered with mud, and for the next five days we ran two miles every morning, negotiated obstacle courses, climbed rocks, kayaked, canoed and laughed each other to sleep as we bullshitted in our tent at night. We trekked through uncharted land, learned what was edible in the woods, perfected mouth-to-mouth resuscitation and kept busy and sore from before dawn until late at night.

We went out on expeditions and rock climbed above the shores of Lake Superior. No amount of fixed rope, jumars or pitons would ever make me hate heights less, but it was exhilarating to learn, shredding knees and elbows as I went. And in the afternoons, we rappelled back down, jumping backward off the cliff and hopping down the rock face.

For our two-week Long Expedition we canoed north across the Canadian border through the great network of lakes and streams that had sustained Indians, trappers, voyageurs in their enormous trading canoes, and missionaries for centuries. It was beautiful, rolling country, filled with evergreens and birch trees, wild animals and the calls of birds.

As we paddled farther from American waters the portage trails narrowed and were merely marked by a single blaze made by a ranger with his hatchet on the trunk of a tree. The Canadian water was clean and pure for swimming and drinking. We shared it with no one else we saw, only the trees, beavers, deer, hawk, bear and jays who crossed our paths, and the loons we heard uttering their many voiced, fantastic cries late into the northern nights.

We came up Moose Lake to Birch Lake, through Knife Lake and across the Sangemon into Ross Lake. We portaged into Dart Lake because a stream had dried up, and twice I had to be pulled out of thigh deep mud as the weight of the canoe gunnels on my shoulders drove me down. At least I was heading in the right direction as opposed to those portages where you followed a wrong turn someone had beaten into the bushes the week before and went two miles before realizing it with a ninety pound pack or a canoe bearing down on your shoulders, inching up twelve foot rock inclines on severely scraped knees and then burrowing under a giant fallen tree a little ways up across the trail, belly on the muddy forest floor, squirming forward, until you finally figured out the only way out was to head back precisely whence you'd come.

Then came the climactic Outward Bound experience, the Solo. Five days out, after rising and breaking camp before sun up (for some reason more than twice as much as the average day's canoeing gets done in the morning, so long as you start early), and paddling hard, the canoe stroke becoming a kind of mantra, our instructor met us at an island camp site in the middle of Pickerel Lake. We stowed our gear there, and the next morning he deposited each of us at an isolated stretch of shore around the lake's perimeter. This was home for the next four days. You had a cup for sipping water, a fish hook and string, a book of matches, and a tarpaulin in case it rained. I was situated on a small point, from which I commanded a wide view of the water. Friendly ants rallied around along with monster mosquitoes. By four in the morning the mosquitoes were so thick and noisy I restarted the fire. When I awoke in the dawn it was to find a family of partridge munching breakfast no more than twenty feet away. The day broke gusty and clear, and I spent hours fishing with my hand line without ever coming close to a strike.

Four days of absolute solitude, a diet of six blueberries picked each day, two swims and unlimited water. I remember beautiful golden sunsets, singing many previously forgotten songs, watching my tentmates swim and the smoke rise from their fires around the lake, living a life apart. I thought, then, of Father Hilary. Was this what he was after?

When, after the fourth day, our instructors canoed us back to the island camp site, we ate a big pot of spaghetti, very slowly. Then we feasted on three apple pies, sharing our adventures as we chewed. The next day we struggled on obscure Canadian streams, often missing even more obscure landmarks, overgrown portage trails and unmarked short cuts. But we peresevered until we reached Kashipiwi Lake, farther north than any human settlement between us and the Yukon, and that made it all worthwhile.

On the homeward leg of our journey a great black storm rose up on Basswood Lake. Waves began breaking against the canoe, and my two crewmen were exhausted and beginning to get sick. We shipped water and nearly capsized twice, but made it to the Ranger station on the American side of the Canadian border as the sun broke through the clouds. The Ranger's wife rewarded our return with brownies fresh from her oven. That night we made it into camp in time to dry our clothes, eat a hot meal, sleep beneath the stars, and remember the majesty of all we had paddled through.

"I am glad," wrote Aldo Leopold, "I shall never be young without wild country to be young in. Of what avail are forty freedoms without a blank spot on the map?"

I came away from Outward Bound with a sense of possibility, even optimism, restored. But for all that, it was great just for being able to write to Tommy:

And if you ever paddle a full day—from seven in the morning until seven at night—and having gone near forty miles over eleven lakes, three rivers, and fifteen portages, running rapids with water swirling and spraying around you, struggling to stay in the clearest channel down, running up on rock so badly everyone in the canoe has to jump out whether the water was trickling at your ankles or exploding at your chin until you finally get through the worst and sweep back into the river's gentle flow, and sure the wind can blow up and raise white caps three feet high, and the canoe can bend and fill so fast and roll among the swells so that you have to angle it through, six arms straining but staying on because nothing is worse in rough weather than turning back...

If you have done all that and then gotten out onto a fair-sized lake around sunset and pulled into a middling sized island with a fine campsite and plenty of exposure to the breeze, landed and pulled up the canoes, hauled up your packs and began to figure out the day's big meal, collecting firewood, soaping the pots, on the outside as well as the inside to make sure the black comes off more easily after cooking, set up the tents, being careful the guy lines are pulled up as tight as piano strings and the fly tarp is utterly secure so that even a big bout of thunder and lightning and whipping wind along with a righteous rain couldn't drown it out, and when you finished all that you stripped your dampened shirt and your soggy trousers, and soaked boots and permanently wet socks and jumped into the lukewarm lake and then scouted around and found a high rock above a rockless bottom and jumped fifteen maybe twenty feet, making a joyous splash, and swam into shore and began to soap up your own body, unsure of what was sun tan and what was dirt, and dove back into the lake to rinse off and then laid down on a big old warm rock and watched the setting sun begin to descend...

Then you tugged on your shorts and dry socks and sneakers, and pretty soon the chicken noodle soup was served, and you got a big bowl of it and savored it, and then you filled the bowl with tuna casserole with peas and a touch of cheese that tasted even better, and you sat down next to a bunch of friends you had only met three weeks before but now seemed as close as the closest friends you had ever had, feeling warm from the fire and the food and the talk of the day gone by, and by and by began talking about tomorrow and next week until you were telling someone you had never met a month ago what it was you hoped to be doing for the rest of your life, and there you were somewhere way up in Canada leading as simple a life as you could imagine as the fire crackled and the loons began to cry, and the sun set and you took a last look at the sky all lit up gold and helped yourself to a cup of cocoa which warmed you all over again, and you climbed into a pair of baggy dry trousers and put on your turtleneck and began to sing with the rest of the brigade, sitting around the campfire, when the wind came up and the air turned crisp and the mosquitoes were too cold to bite, and someone decided that this was a good night to pop popcorn, and the pot was greased and the kernels thrown in, and they popped quickly because of the blazing fire, and everyone had handful until soon another pot was popping, as you sang, "Swing Low, Sweet Chariot," or "Folsom Prison," or "There but for Fortune," and you could not measure the great feeling of warmth in degrees so much as in the shared fellowship of a hard day, and the prospect of doing it all over again tomorrow...

Then, as the fire begins to die some of the guys head for the tents, but after you help finish up with the cleaning and the packing, you notice that the sky is clear, and if you look closely you can catch a glimmer of the northern lights, as well as bundles of other stars across the sky, and so you drag your sleeping bag from your tent and lay it out on a bed of pine needles overlooking the lake, and strip down naked and climb into it and feel the softness and the warmth and relish the comfort more than any mattress in any room at home and say goodnight to all the others, and busy yourself with your own thoughts—the next morning's oat meal, a better way to "J" stroke, where you'll be tomorrow night, and soon you begin to think of home and a pretty girl whose brown eyes are so soft and whose lips are warm and wet to kiss, and whose body curls into your body, and you think about her and you look into the star-filled sky, and you feel the cool breeze blowing on your forehead and your cheeks, and as you fall to sleep you wish that she were with you here, because then you know you'd never come back.

And when we made our way back to the main camp, lo and behold, I found a note under my pillow, addressed "To the Guy Who Slept Here Last Night:"

> Congratulations on your safe return. By the time you get this we'll be acting like idiots

in the woods, so enjoy the comfort of this cozy bunk bed with mosquito netting intact, and think of poor me sleeping under the stars. Have a safe trip home, wherever that is—

The Girl Who Slept Here Last Night"

I did think about her, all the way back to New York, what it would be like to meet such a girl, say at the beach, and then see her again at the end of the day on the boardwalk, all alone, and talk to her. And if she were friendly I might even work up the nerve to ask her to the movies, and I would think, yeah, maybe she did like me, and I even enjoyed the silences between us and didn't want to fill them up with anything except the sheer pleasure of feeling her sit next to me....

So I thought, but the truth of the matter is that even as I indulged in these calf love day dreams of a multi-formed madonna voyageuring in the North Woods, the note I left her in return was pathetic, and if she ever got it, I never heard from her.

There was one more lunkhead move I had to endure. One day that August an older Outward Bound and Long Island friend and I went gliding and rock climbing in the Hudson Highlands near New Paltz. Afterwards we picnicked by a pretty little stream and went through a half gallon jug of Napa Sonoma Mendocino rot gut red wine. Driving back down to Long Island Jimmy Bernuth began reminiscing about his days in the Peace Corps in Sierra Leone, and as we passed Kennedy Airport, asked, "Do you want to go to Africa?" I nodded and suddenly we were inside the Pan Am building scouting flights, the closest to Africa being one for Lisbon. Using our Outward Bound skills, we bypassed the ticket counter and clambered up and over a seven foot retaining wall to get to the gangway. The stewardesses looked quite nervous but said nothing as we entered the plane in our mud and wine-stained L.L. Bean climbing clothes, so we marched to the back and sat down.

In due course two men in patterned sports jackets and loud ties came on aboard and approached us. One had a conspicuous bulge at precisely the spot where a shoulder holster might have fit. After what we considered some eloquent, but ultimately futile verbal pyrotechnics, we were led off the plane, hand cuffed, taken to the airport precinct station and charged with soliciting fares and attempted hijacking. The final humiliation came when Jim's parents were out to dinner, and my poor mother had to drive over in the dark to bail us out. Later

Jimmy's father said to me, not unkindly, "Jamie, that stunt you and Jimmy pulled…that was a fuckin' stupid thing to do."

In the finale of this misadventure we appeared in Queens traffic court in front of an exasperated Italian-American judge, who, upon learning that Jim would be joining the CUNY faculty that Fall and I was entering Johns Hopkins, reduced the charges to disorderly conduct and fined us $10 apiece. "Fellas, wise up," he said by way of admonition before moving on to the next case. I tried. I'm still trying.

Still, Outward Bound had made its mark on me, and I was ready to move on, to college and into the 1970s, wherever they led.

Acknowledgements

Some characters have been conflated, and some names have been changed to protect the innocent, wherever they may be.

Father Hilary's remarks on Renaissance artists in the first chapter of "1970" were largely drawn from my former Scribners' colleague Jacques Barzun's magisterial *From Dawn to Decadence*.

About the Author

James P. MacGuire was born in New York and educated at Johns Hopkins and Cambridge. After serving as country program director of Catholic Relief Services in Burundi, he has worked at Time Inc., Macmillan, The Health Network, and the Corporation for Public Broadcasting. His poetry, fiction and journalism have appeared in many national publications.

He is the author or co-author of fourteen books and two beloved sons, Pierce and Rhoads. MacGuire lives in New York with the sublime Michelle Coppedge.

Made in the USA
Coppell, TX
21 April 2021